W9-BJK-529

EASY COOKING

Canadian Living's™ best

BY
Elizabeth Baird

AND

The Food Writers of Canadian Living Magazine
and The Canadian Living Test Kitchen

A MADISON PRESS BOOK
PRODUCED FOR
BALLANTINE BOOKS AND CANADIAN LIVING™

Copyright © 1995 by Telemedia Communications Inc.
and The Madison Press Limited.

All rights reserved. No part of this publication may be reproduced,
stored in a retrieval system, or transmitted in any form or by any means,
electronic, mechanical, photocopying, recording or otherwise,
without prior permission of the publishers.

Ballantine Books
A Division of
Random House of
Canada Limited
1265 Aerowood Drive
Mississauga, Ontario
Canada
L4W 1B9

Canadian Living
Telemedia
Communications Inc.
25 Sheppard Avenue West
Suite 100
North York, Ontario
Canada
M2N 6S7

Canadian Cataloguing in Publication Data

Easy cooking

(Canadian Living's best)
Includes index.
ISBN 0-345-39805-X

1. Quick and easy cookery.   2. Cookery.
I. Title.   II. Series.

TX833.5.B35 1995   641.5'12   C95-930520-3

™Canadian Living is a trademark owned by
Telemedia Communications Inc. and licensed by The Madison Press Limited.
All trademark rights, registered and unregistered, are reserved worldwide.

EDITORIAL DIRECTOR: Hugh Brewster
PROJECT EDITOR: Wanda Nowakowska
EDITORIAL ASSISTANCE: Beverley Renahan
PRODUCTION DIRECTOR: Susan Barrable
PRODUCTION COORDINATOR: Donna Chong
BOOK DESIGN AND LAYOUT: Gordon Sibley Design Inc.
COLOR SEPARATION: Colour Technologies
PRINTING AND BINDING: Friesen Printers

CANADIAN LIVING ADVISORY BOARD: Elizabeth Baird, Bonnie Baker Cowan,
Anna Hobbs, Caren King, Greg MacNeil

CANADIAN LIVING'S™ BEST EASY COOKING
was produced by Madison Press Books
under the direction of Albert E. Cummings

Madison Press Books
40 Madison Avenue
Toronto, Ontario, Canada
M5R 2S1

Printed in Canada

Contents

Introduction 5

Quick Suppers 6

Easy Entertaining 40

Desserts on the Double...................... 58

Breakfast & Lunch 74

Credits 90

Index 92

Introduction

Being able to put a delicious meal on the table quickly and efficiently makes all the difference in a busy day. But just what is cooking that's easy enough to fit into our active lives?

First of all, it's fast. Most of the recipes you'll find here can be prepared, cooked and served in half an hour or less. Or, you can relax with a no-tend dinner that takes just minutes to put together and then unwind or do other things while it cooks or cools to delicious perfection.

Less preparation and cooking time also means fewer ingredients — most of which you can find at your local supermarket, including popular new ingredients like capers, hoisin sauce and tortillas. As well, supermarket produce, meat, fish and poultry are now packaged so they're ready for the pot or grill as soon as you unwrap them.

And when the cooking is easy, so are the techniques. In *Canadian Living's Best Easy Cooking*, you'll find streamlined cooking methods that are simple and logical to follow. And the equipment is basic, too — a good skillet, roasting pan, heavy-bottomed saucepans, a good knife and chopping board are all you need.

Whether you choose a quick weeknight supper, a three-ingredient dessert or an impressive dinner-party dish, we know you'll be delighted with how pleasurable — and easy! — good cooking can be.

Elizabeth Baird

Spicy Noodle Salad
(recipe, p. 34)

Quick Suppers

The best weeknight suppers are the ones everyone in the family enjoys — and requests over and over again! It's a bonus when these suppers are quick to prepare, with short ingredient lists and cooking methods easy enough for helpers to join in.

Steak and Harvest Vegetable Fajitas ▶

Avocados give these colorful fajitas an extra hit of smooth flavor. Serve with light sour cream — then step back and enjoy the stampede to the supper table!

1 lb	sirloin steak	500 g
1-1/2 tsp	chili powder	7 mL
3/4 tsp	each salt and pepper	4 mL
2 tbsp	vegetable oil	25 mL
1	onion, sliced	1
4	cloves garlic, minced	4
1 tsp	ground cumin	5 mL
Pinch	hot pepper flakes	Pinch
1	each sweet red, green and yellow pepper, thinly sliced	1
1	zucchini, halved lengthwise and sliced	1
1 tsp	Dijon mustard	5 mL
2 tbsp	chopped fresh coriander (optional)	25 mL
6	10-inch (25 cm) flour tortillas	6
2	avocados	2
1/3 cup	lime juice	75 mL

● Trim any fat from steak; slice steak into thin strips. In bowl, toss steak with chili powder and 1/4 tsp (1 mL) each of the salt and pepper.

● In large nonstick skillet, heat 1 tbsp (15 mL) of the oil over medium-high heat; cook steak, in batches and stirring, for 2-1/2 minutes or until browned. Remove to plate.

● Add remaining oil to skillet; cook onion, half of the garlic, the cumin, hot pepper flakes and 1/4 tsp (5 mL) each of the salt and pepper, stirring, for 3 minutes.

● Add sweet peppers and zucchini; cook, stirring, for 3 minutes or until tender-crisp. Return meat to skillet; add mustard, and coriander (if using) and toss gently.

● Meanwhile, wrap tortillas in foil; heat in 350°F (180°C) oven for 5 minutes or until warmed through.

● Peel and pit avocados; mash with lime juice and remaining garlic, salt and pepper.

● Spread 2 tbsp (25 mL) avocado mixture over tortillas. Divide beef mixture among tortillas and roll up. Serve with remaining avocado mixture. Makes 6 servings.

TIP: To avoid bruised avocados, buy them a few days ahead and choose hard, green specimens. Let them ripen at room temperature, in a single layer out of the sun, for 3 or 4 days or until they yield to the touch.

THE BASICS — FAST!

You don't have to be a fledgling cook to wonder just how much to use or how long to cook basic sides such as rice, pasta or even potatoes. So here it is, a handy reference to make cooking easier for the whole household.

DRIED PASTA

20 cups	water	5 L
2 tbsp	salt	25 mL
1 lb	dried pasta	500 g

● In large covered pot, bring water and salt to full rolling boil. Stir in pasta, separating pieces; return to boil and boil, uncovered and stirring occasionally, for 8 to 10 minutes or until tender but firm. Drain well. Makes 4 servings.

FRESH PASTA

16 cups	water	4 L
4 tsp	salt	20 mL
1 lb	fresh pasta	500 g

● In large covered pot, bring water and salt to full rolling boil. Stir in pasta, separating pieces; return to boil and boil, uncovered and stirring occasionally, for 1 to 3 minutes or until tender but firm. Drain well. Makes 4 servings.

RICE

1-1/3 cups	water	325 mL
Pinch	salt	Pinch
2/3 cup	white or brown long grain rice	150 mL

● In saucepan, bring water and salt to boil; stir in rice. Cover and reduce heat to low; simmer white rice for 20 minutes, brown rice for 40 minutes, or until rice is tender and liquid absorbed. Makes 2 cups (500 mL), enough for 2 servings.

TIP: Chicken or vegetable stock can be substituted for water. Omit salt if stock is salted.

BOILED POTATOES

● Scrub or peel potatoes; place in large pot. Cover with boiling water; add salt (about 1 tsp/2 mL for 2 lb/1 kg potatoes). Cover and bring to boil; boil for about 20 minutes or until fork-tender. Drain and return to pot over low heat for 30 seconds to evaporate excess moisture.

MASHED POTATOES

2 lb	hot boiled peeled potatoes (4 potatoes)	1 kg
1 cup	buttermilk or milk	250 mL
4 tsp	butter	20 mL
1/2 tsp	each salt and pepper	2 mL

● In pot, mash together potatoes, buttermilk, butter, salt and pepper until smooth. Makes 4 servings.

KASHA

1 cup	kasha	250 mL
1	egg	1
1/2 tsp	salt	2 mL
Pinch	pepper	Pinch
1-1/2 cups	boiling water	375 mL
1 tbsp	butter	15 mL

● In saucepan, combine kasha, egg, salt and pepper; cook over medium-low heat, stirring, for 3 minutes or until dry and kernels separate. Stir in water and butter; cover and cook, without stirring, for 10 to 12 minutes or until water is absorbed. Fluff with fork. Makes 1-1/2 cups (375 mL), enough for 2 servings.

POLENTA

4 cups	water	1 L
1/2 tsp	salt	2 mL
1 cup	cornmeal	250 mL

● In large saucepan, bring water and salt to boil over high heat; reduce heat to low. Gradually whisk in cornmeal; cook, stirring often with wooden spoon, for 20 to 25 minutes or until thick enough to mound. Makes 3-1/2 cups (875 mL), enough for 4 servings.

BARLEY

2 cups	water or vegetable or chicken stock	500 mL
1/4 tsp	salt	1 mL
1 cup	pot or pearl barley	250 mL

● In saucepan, bring water and salt to boil over high heat; stir in barley. Reduce heat to low; cover and simmer for 40 minutes or until tender and liquid has evaporated. Makes 3 cups (750 mL), enough for 4 servings.

COUSCOUS

1-1/2 cups	water or vegetable or chicken stock	375 mL
Pinch	salt	Pinch
1 cup	couscous	250 mL

● In saucepan, bring water and salt to boil; stir in couscous. Remove from heat; cover and let stand for 5 minutes. Fluff with fork. Makes 3 cups (750 mL), enough for 4 servings.

Beef and Vegetable Stir-Fry for One ▲

1 tbsp	packed brown sugar	15 mL
1 tbsp	each wine vinegar and soy sauce	15 mL
1 tsp	cornstarch	5 mL
4 oz	round steak	125 g
2 tsp	vegetable oil	10 mL
2 cups	frozen Oriental-style mixed vegetables	500 mL
Quarter	pkg (350 g) steamed Chinese noodles, broken up	Quarter

● In small bowl, stir together sugar, vinegar, soy sauce, cornstarch and 1 tbsp (15 mL) water until cornstarch is dissolved; set aside.

● Trim fat from steak; cut meat diagonally into thin slices. In nonstick skillet, heat half of the oil over medium-high heat; cook meat, stirring, for 2 to 3 minutes or until well browned. Remove to plate.

● Add remaining oil and vegetables to pan; stir-fry for 5 to 6 minutes or until tender. Stir cornstarch mixture; stir into pan along with meat. Cook, stirring, until sauce is boiling and thickened. Add noodles; cook until heated through. Makes 1 serving.

The produce section of supermarkets now includes many new items — tofu, salad dressings and, most recently, vacuum-packed steamed Chinese noodles that need only minutes to heat through. In a pinch, cooked spaghetti can be substituted.

Steak Pizzaiola

In Italian, "alla pizzaiola" means that the dish is cooked in a sauce that has all the popular tastes of pizza — tomatoes, onion and oregano. Serve with rice, plain pasta or mashed potatoes and a crunchy green vegetable such as beans or sugar snap peas.

1 lb	boneless sirloin steak	500 g
1/2 tsp	salt	2 mL
1/4 tsp	pepper	1 mL
2 tbsp	olive oil	25 mL
1	onion, thinly sliced	1
3	cloves garlic, minced	3
2	large tomatoes, peeled, seeded and chopped	2
2 tbsp	chopped fresh oregano	25 mL

● Between sheets of waxed paper, pound steak with meat mallet to just under 1/4-inch (5 mm) thickness. Cut into 1/2-inch (1 cm) wide strips; season with pinch each of the salt and pepper.

● In large skillet, heat oil over high heat; brown meat, in batches, for 2 minutes. Remove to plate.

● Reduce heat to medium. Add onion and garlic; cook, stirring, for about 5 minutes or until softened. Stir in tomatoes, oregano and remaining salt and pepper, stirring to scrape up brown bits.

● Return meat and any accumulated juices to pan; simmer for 5 minutes or until sauce is slightly thickened and meat is tender. Makes 4 servings.

TIP: If you don't have a meat mallet, pound the steak with the side of a metal pie plate or the bottom of a small heavy saucepan or skillet.

Lean and Saucy Swiss Steak ▶

Noodles or rice make an ideal bed for a serving of this lightened-up family favorite.

3 tbsp	all-purpose flour	50 mL
	Salt and pepper	
1 lb	lean cube steak, cut into 4 pieces	500 g
4 tsp	vegetable oil	20 mL
1	large onion, thinly sliced	1
3	carrots, thinly sliced	3
2	cloves garlic, minced	2
3/4 tsp	dried oregano	4 mL
1/2 tsp	granulated sugar	2 mL
1	can (14 oz/398 mL) stewed tomatoes	1
1 tbsp	red wine vinegar	15 mL
	Chopped fresh parsley	

● In shallow dish, combine flour and pinch each salt and pepper; dredge steak in mixture. Reserve flour.

● In nonstick skillet, heat 2 tsp (10 mL) of the oil over medium-high heat; cook steak for about 2 minutes on each side or until browned. Remove to plate.

● Add remaining oil, onion, carrots, garlic and 1 tbsp (15 mL) water to pan; cover and cook over medium heat, stirring often, for 6 minutes or until vegetables are softened. Stir in reserved flour, oregano, sugar, 1/2 tsp (2 mL) pepper and 1/4 tsp (1 mL) salt; cook for 1 minute. Pour in tomatoes and vinegar; bring to boil, stirring to scrape up brown bits.

● Return meat to pan; reduce heat, cover and simmer for 20 minutes or until tender. Uncover and simmer for 2 minutes or until thickened. Season with salt and pepper to taste. Garnish with parsley. Makes 4 servings.

Teriyaki Pork Burgers ▲

Lean ground pork, flavored with ginger and teriyaki and crunchy with water chestnuts, sizzles to perfection on the grill. Sliced red onion, tomatoes, pickled hot pepper rings or sweet peppers all make great toppers.

1	egg	1
1	clove garlic, minced	1
1/4 cup	dry bread crumbs	50 mL
1/4 cup	chopped water chestnuts	50 mL
2 tbsp	chopped green onion	25 mL
2 tbsp	teriyaki sauce	25 mL
2 tsp	chopped fresh gingerroot	10 mL
1-1/2 tsp	dry mustard	7 mL
1/4 tsp	each salt and pepper	1 mL
1 lb	lean ground pork	500 g
6	hamburger buns	6

● In bowl, beat egg; mix in garlic, bread crumbs, water chestnuts, onion, teriyaki sauce, ginger, mustard, salt and pepper. Mix in pork; shape into six 3/4-inch (2 cm) thick patties.

● Place patties on greased grill over medium-high heat; cook, turning once, for 12 to 14 minutes or until no longer pink inside. Sandwich in buns. Makes 6 servings.

Chick-Pea Burgers

1	can (19 oz/540 mL) chick-peas, drained and rinsed	1
1 cup	cooked rice	250 mL
1/3 cup	each grated onion, carrot and zucchini	75 mL
1/4 cup	dry bread crumbs	50 mL
1	egg, beaten	1
1	clove garlic, minced	1
2 tbsp	tahini or peanut butter	25 mL
1 tbsp	lemon juice	15 mL
1/2 tsp	salt	2 mL
1/4 tsp	each pepper and dry mustard	1 mL
3	pita breads	3

● In large bowl and using potato masher, mash chick-peas coarsely; stir in rice, onion, carrot, zucchini, bread crumbs, egg, garlic, tahini, lemon juice, salt, pepper and mustard. Shape into six 3/4-inch (2 cm) thick patties.

● Place patties on greased grill over medium-high heat; cook, turning once, for about 10 minutes or until golden brown. Halve pita breads and pull open to form pockets; insert burger into each. Makes 6 servings.

A grain-and-legume burger is a timely barbecue item for vegetarians, and a tasty alternative to meat burgers. Pack into pita bread along with alfalfa sprouts and tomato and Spanish onion slices.

Lemony Chicken Burgers

1	egg	1
1/4 cup	dry bread crumbs	50 mL
1	small onion, grated	1
2 tbsp	chopped fresh chives or green onion	25 mL
1 tbsp	grated lemon rind	15 mL
1 tbsp	lemon juice	15 mL
1 tbsp	water	15 mL
2 tsp	Dijon mustard	10 mL
1/2 tsp	salt	2 mL
1/4 tsp	pepper	1 mL
1 lb	lean ground chicken	500 g
6	hamburger buns	6

● In bowl, beat egg; mix in bread crumbs, onion, chives, lemon rind and juice, water, mustard, salt and pepper. Mix in chicken; shape into six 3/4-inch (2 cm) thick patties.

● Place patties on greased grill over medium-high heat; cook, turning once, for 12 to 14 minutes or until no longer pink inside. Sandwich in buns. Makes 6 servings.

You'll find these fresh-tasting burgers a little moist to pat into shape (dipping your hands into water helps) but they firm up nicely on the grill and are crowd pleasers stuffed into buns and topped with sweet pepper rings.

FOUR WAYS TO MAKE A BURGER — THE BEST!

1 Good burgers usually contain an egg to hold the patties together, along with some water or juice. This added moisture is especially important when using lean ground meats and poultry.

2 Instead of chopping onions, grate them for a moist burger that holds together better on the grill. One small onion yields about 1/4 cup (50 mL) grated.

3 Buttered buns? No way. Try some of the specialty mustards like Dijon or Russian-style. Or, spread buns with light mayonnaise, herbed cream cheese or trendy tapenade, guacamole or pesto.

4 Ketchup and relish? Sure, but why not showcase some of your own preserves — corn or zucchini relish, bread and butter pickles, sliced sweet and hot pickled pepper, chutneys, salsa or chili sauce.

Burgerbobs in a Bun ◄

1	egg	1
1/4 cup	dry bread crumbs	50 mL
1/4 cup	ketchup	50 mL
1 tsp	Worcestershire sauce	5 mL
1 tsp	Dijon mustard	5 mL
1/2 tsp	salt	2 mL
1/4 tsp	pepper	1 mL
1 lb	lean ground beef	500 g
1	zucchini	1
4	submarine buns	4

● In bowl, beat egg; mix in bread crumbs, ketchup, Worcestershire sauce, mustard, salt and pepper. Mix in beef; shape into 12 meatballs.

● Cut zucchini into 16 slices. Beginning with zucchini, alternately thread 4 zucchini and 3 meatballs onto each skewer.

● Place on greased grill over medium heat; cook, carefully turning once, for 10 to 15 minutes or until meatballs are no longer pink inside. Slide kabobs off skewers into buns. Makes 4 servings.

Submarine buns cradle a skewer of golden-crisp meatballs and tender zucchini slices. Add a bowl of greens tossed with a tangy vinaigrette.

Lamb Curry

2 lb	lamb shoulder	1 kg
2 tbsp	curry powder	25 mL
1 tbsp	lime juice	15 mL
1 tsp	vegetable oil	5 mL
2	onions, chopped	2
3	cloves garlic, minced	3
2 tsp	minced gingerroot	10 mL
2 tbsp	all-purpose flour	25 mL
3 cups	chicken stock	750 mL
1/4 cup	tomato paste	50 mL
1/4 cup	chopped fresh coriander or parsley	50 mL
	Salt and pepper	
6 cups	hot cooked rice	1.5 L

● Cut lamb into 1-inch (2.5 cm) pieces. In large bowl, combine curry powder and lime juice; add lamb and toss to coat well.

● In deep nonstick skillet, heat oil over medium-high heat; brown lamb on all sides. Add onions, garlic and ginger; cook, stirring, for about 5 minutes or until onions are softened. Sprinkle with flour; cook, stirring, for 1 minute.

● Whisk in stock and tomato paste; bring to simmer, stirring. Reduce heat to medium; cover and cook for 1-1/2 hours or until lamb is tender. Stir in coriander; cook for 2 minutes. Season with salt and pepper to taste. Serve over rice. Makes 6 servings.

This is a gentle curried lamb, one that's nicely complemented by chutney, chopped pears, toasted nuts and thick yogurt. Serve over rice — aromatic basmati, if available.

Microwave Beef-Topped Tostadas ▼

Serve this open-faced Mexican-style sandwich with light sour cream and/or salsa.

TIP: Flour tortillas are available in most supermarkets across Canada. Look for them in the refrigerator or frozen food section.

4	large flour tortillas	4
1 lb	lean ground beef	500 g
1	onion, chopped	1
1	jalapeño pepper, seeded and diced	1
1	clove garlic, minced	1
1 tbsp	chili powder	15 mL
1 tsp	ground cumin	5 mL
1/4 tsp	salt	1 mL
Pinch	pepper	Pinch
1	large tomato, seeded and chopped	1
1 cup	shredded lettuce	250 mL
1 cup	shredded Cheddar cheese	250 mL

● Pierce tortillas in a few places; microwave each at High, turning and rotating once, for 1-1/2 to 2 minutes or until barely crisp. Place on microwaveable plates.

● In 8-cup (2 L) microwaveable bowl, crumble beef; add onion, jalapeño pepper and garlic. Microwave at High, stirring often, for 3 to 5 minutes or until meat is no longer pink; stir in chili powder, cumin, salt and pepper.

● Add tomato; microwave at High for 1 to 2 minutes or until hot. Using slotted spoon, divide among tortillas; sprinkle with lettuce, then Cheddar. Microwave each at High for 30 to 60 seconds or until Cheddar melts. Makes 4 servings.

Mellow Liver and Onions

3 tbsp	vegetable oil	50 mL
6	onions, sliced	6
1/2 tsp	dried sage	2 mL
1/4 tsp	(approx) each salt and pepper	1 mL
1 lb	calves' or beef liver (1/2 inch/1 cm thick)	500 g
1/4 cup	all-purpose flour	50 mL
1/2 cup	beef stock	125 mL
2 tbsp	balsamic or red wine vinegar	25 mL
1-1/2 tsp	granulated sugar	7 mL
	Chopped fresh parsley	

● In large heavy skillet, heat 1 tbsp (15 mL) of the oil over medium heat; cook onions and sage, stirring often, for 8 minutes or until softened. Reduce heat to medium-low; cook, stirring occasionally, for 20 minutes or until deep golden. Season with salt and pepper to taste. Remove and keep warm.

● Meanwhile, trim any membranes and connective tissue from liver. In shallow dish, combine flour and 1/4 tsp (1 mL) each salt and pepper. Wipe out skillet; heat remaining oil over medium-high heat.

● Dredge liver in flour mixture to coat, shaking off excess; add to skillet and cook, in batches if necessary and turning once, for 2 to 4 minutes or until browned, slightly pink inside and still springy to the touch. Remove to heated plates.

● Add stock, vinegar and sugar to pan; bring to boil, stirring to scrape up brown bits. Boil, stirring, for 1 to 2 minutes or until reduced to about 1/3 cup (75 mL). Mound onions over liver; top with sauce. Sprinkle with parsley. Makes 4 servings.

TIP: Liver, like all variety meats, is very perishable; use on the day of purchase or by the next day at the latest.

If liver is one of those childhood horror dishes, why is it one of the most popular restaurant grill choices? The answer lies in the quality of the liver (we suggest calves' or baby beef) and in the way it's cooked. In the pan too long or over too high heat, and liver could resole shoes. But, with a quick cook in the pan until golden on the outside and still slightly pink inside, liver is fork-tender bliss.

Chili Meat Loaf Muffins

1 lb	lean ground beef	500 g
3/4 cup	medium salsa	175 mL
1 tsp	chili powder	5 mL
1/2 tsp	salt	2 ml
1/4 tsp	pepper	1 mL
1	can (14 oz/398 mL) red kidney beans, drained and rinsed	
1/2 cup	shredded Monterey Jack or Cheddar cheese	125 mL

● In bowl, break up beef with fork; mix in 1/4 cup (50 mL) of the salsa, chili powder, salt and pepper.

● Divide into 8 portions; place in muffin cups. Press center of each to form well 3/4 inch (2 cm) deep and 1-1/2 inches (4 cm) wide. Bake in 400°F (200°C) oven for 10 minutes or until firm to the touch and no longer pink inside.

● Combine kidney beans and remaining salsa; spoon into wells. Sprinkle with cheese. Bake for 7 to 8 minutes or until beans are hot and cheese has melted. Using two forks, remove from muffin cups. Makes 4 servings.

Beans and salsa cupped in ground beef and baked under melting cheese spell a fun dish kids are sure to enjoy. Start some potatoes baking in the oven while the muffins are being assembled, then let meat and potatoes bake while you grate carrots and shred cabbage for a slaw.

Fruited Pork Chops with Squash ▶

With golden autumn colors and harvest-fresh flavors, this dish is a tasty celebration of fall. Choose an easy-to-peel squash such as butternut or Delicata, or pick an acorn squash and leave the skin on for color contrast. If you like, add a sliced, cored apple to the skillet, at the same time as the squash.

4	pork loin chops	4
1/2 tsp	salt	2 mL
1/4 tsp	pepper	1 mL
1 tsp	vegetable oil	5 mL
1	onion, diced	1
1-1/2 cups	apple cider or juice	375 mL
2-1/2 cups	thinly sliced peeled squash (about half a squash)	625 mL
1/4 cup	sliced dried apricots	50 mL

● Trim fat from chops; sprinkle with salt and pepper.

● In large heavy skillet, heat oil over medium-high heat; cook chops for 3 to 4 minutes on each side or until browned. Remove and set aside.

● Add onion to pan; cook over medium heat, stirring occasionally and adding 1 tbsp (15 mL) water if necessary to prevent sticking, for about 5 minutes or until softened.

● Pour in apple cider, stirring to scrape up brown bits. Add squash and apricots; cover and simmer for 7 to 8 minutes or until squash is tender.

● Return chops to pan; cook for 3 to 5 minutes or just until no longer pink inside. Makes 4 servings.

TIP: Slash the rounded edge of pork chops at 1-inch (2.5 cm) intervals to prevent chops from curling.

Peppers Aplenty Pork Chops

Let summer's bounty supply the sweet red, yellow and green peppers for this fast skillet supper — featured on our cover.

4	pork loin chops	4
1 tbsp	paprika	15 mL
1 tbsp	vegetable oil	15 mL
1	large onion, sliced	1
1	clove garlic, minced	1
1	each sweet red, yellow and green pepper, sliced	1
1	large tomato, chopped	1
1 tsp	caraway seeds	5 mL
1	bay leaf	1
1/2 tsp	salt	2 mL
1/4 tsp	pepper	1 mL

● Trim fat from chops; rub with half of the paprika. In large nonstick skillet, heat oil over medium-high heat; cook chops for 3 to 4 minutes on each side or until browned.

● Add remaining paprika, onion, garlic and sweet peppers; cook, stirring occasionally, for 4 minutes or until vegetables are softened.

● Add tomato, caraway seeds, bay leaf, salt and pepper, tossing together well; cover and cook over medium heat for 12 to 15 minutes or until juicy, peppers are tender and chops are no longer pink inside. Discard bay leaf. Makes 4 servings.

Chicken Stew for Two

Cooking for one or two can be a challenge, especially if you don't want perpetual leftovers. A fresh chicken stew, though, is quick and very tasty. Serve over hot biscuits or extra potatoes.

2	boneless skinless chicken breasts	2
2 tbsp	all-purpose flour	25 mL
1/4 tsp	each dried thyme and paprika	1 mL
1/4 tsp	(approx) salt and pepper	1 mL
2 tsp	vegetable oil	10 mL
1	onion, chopped	1
2 cups	chicken stock	500 mL
1	potato, peeled and cubed	1
2 cups	frozen mixed vegetables	500 mL
1/4 cup	chopped fresh parsley	50 mL

● Cut chicken into 2-inch (5 cm) cubes. In shallow dish, combine flour, thyme, paprika, salt and pepper; dredge chicken in flour mixture.

● In deep nonstick skillet, heat oil over medium-high heat; cook chicken for about 5 minutes or until browned. Remove chicken and set aside.

● Add onion to pan; cook, stirring often, for about 4 minutes or until softened. Stir in stock; cook, stirring, for 5 minutes or until slightly thickened.

● Return chicken to pan. Add potato; cover and cook over medium heat for 6 minutes. Add frozen vegetables; cook, covered, for 4 to 5 minutes or until vegetables are tender and chicken is no longer pink inside. Stir in parsley; cook for 1 minute. Season with salt and pepper to taste. Makes 2 servings.

TIP: Dredging is simply coating food lightly, often with seasoned flour or crumbs. Here's how: combine the dry ingredients in a shallow dish or paper bag. With tongs, dip the food you want to dredge into the flour mixture in dish, turning to coat all sides. Or, add food, one or two pieces at a time, to bag and shake. To prevent thick coatings, always shake off excess.

Chicken with Hot Peanut Sauce for One

Flavoring sauces are the latest convenience. But when you can whip up your own with so few ingredients and so quickly, why spend the big bucks to buy them? Serve this dish with rice or noodles.

1 tbsp	smooth peanut butter	15 mL
2 tsp	each soy sauce and wine vinegar	10 mL
Pinch	hot pepper flakes	Pinch
1	boneless skinless chicken breast	1
1 tsp	vegetable oil	5 mL
2 tsp	minced garlic	10 mL
1 tsp	minced gingerroot	5 mL

● In measuring cup, stir together 1/4 cup (50 mL) water, peanut butter, soy sauce, vinegar and hot pepper flakes; set aside.

● Cut chicken into 1/2-inch (1 cm) cubes. In nonstick skillet, heat oil over medium-high heat; cook chicken, garlic and ginger, stirring, for 2 to 3 minutes or until chicken is no longer pink inside.

● Stir in peanut butter mixture and bring to boil; reduce heat to low and cook, stirring, for 3 minutes or until thickened. Makes 1 serving.

Chicken Satay

3	boneless skinless chicken breasts	3
2 tbsp	sesame oil	25 mL
1 tbsp	soy sauce	15 mL
1 tbsp	lemon juice	15 mL
1 tsp	minced gingerroot	5 mL
1 tsp	liquid honey	5 mL
2	cloves garlic, minced	2
1/2 tsp	each ground coriander and cumin	2 mL
Pinch	hot pepper flakes	Pinch

● Cut chicken lengthwise into thin strips; thread onto soaked wooden skewers. Place in glass baking dish.

● Whisk together oil, soy sauce, lemon juice, ginger, honey, garlic, coriander, cumin and hot pepper flakes; pour over chicken, turning to coat well. Cover and marinate in refrigerator for 1 hour.

● Reserving marinade, broil chicken or cook on greased grill over high heat, basting occasionally with marinade, for 5 to 6 minutes on each side or until no longer pink inside. Makes 4 servings.

TIP: To prevent scorching, soak wooden skewers in cold water for 30 minutes before threading on chicken and grilling.

Chicken breasts are expensive, especially when they come boned and skinned. You can stretch three into four servings when you cut them into strips and thread them onto skewers.

Quick Chicken and Mushrooms in a Skillet

2 lb	chicken thighs	1 kg
3 tbsp	all-purpose flour	50 mL
2 tbsp	butter	25 mL
1-1/2 cups	sliced mushrooms	375 mL
1	carrot, chopped	1
1	onion, chopped	1
1	clove garlic, minced	1
2 tbsp	chopped fresh thyme (or 2 tsp/10 mL dried)	25 mL
1 tbsp	grated lemon rind	15 mL
1/2 tsp	each salt and pepper	2 mL
1 cup	chicken stock	250 mL
1/4 cup	sour cream	50 mL

● In plastic bag, shake chicken with 2 tbsp (25 mL) of the flour. In nonstick skillet, melt butter over medium-high heat; cook chicken for 15 to 20 minutes or until well browned on all sides and juices run clear when chicken is pierced. Remove to plate.

● Drain off fat from skillet. Add mushrooms, carrot, onion, garlic, thyme, lemon rind, salt and pepper; cook over medium heat, stirring occasionally, for about 10 minutes or until mushrooms are browned.

● Whisk remaining flour into stock; pour into pan and cook, stirring to scrape up brown bits, for 1 to 2 minutes or until thickened. Reduce heat to medium-low; stir in sour cream. Return chicken to pan; cook, without boiling, for 5 minutes or until heated through. Makes 4 to 6 servings.

All in one skillet, this woodsy mushroom chicken dish is easy enough for weeknight dinner yet classy enough for entertaining. Serve with egg noodles richly flecked with chopped parsley and lemon rind.

HOW MUCH CHICKEN TO BUY?
● A pound (500 g) of boneless skinless chicken breasts equals 3 to 4 breasts, depending on size.
● A pound (500 g) of legs is 2 to 3 full legs — drumsticks and thighs.
● For thighs only, count on about 4 to 5 thighs per pound (500 g).

Confetti Chicken Meat Loaf ◄

2 tbsp	vegetable oil	25 mL
2	onions, chopped	2
2	cloves garlic, minced	2
1	each carrot and stalk celery, diced	1
1	each sweet red and green pepper, diced	1
2	eggs	2
1/2 cup	dry bread crumbs	125 mL
1 lb	ground chicken	500 g
1	can (7-1/2 oz/213 mL) tomato sauce	1
1/4 cup	chopped fresh parsley	50 mL
1 tsp	salt	5 mL
1/2 tsp	dried basil	2 mL
1/4 tsp	each pepper and dried thyme	1 mL

● In large skillet, heat oil over medium heat; cook onions, garlic, carrot, celery and sweet peppers, stirring often, for 7 minutes or until softened. Let cool slightly.

● In bowl, combine eggs with bread crumbs. Mix in vegetable mixture, chicken, one-third of the tomato sauce, the parsley, salt, basil, pepper and thyme.

● Line 8- x 4-inch (1.5 L) glass loaf pan with foil, leaving 2-inch (5 cm) overhang. Press meat mixture into pan; spread remaining tomato sauce over top.

● Bake meat loaf in 350°F (180°C) oven for 1-1/2 hours or until meat thermometer inserted in center registers 185°F (85°C) and juices run clear. Let stand in pan for 10 minutes.

● Using foil overhang, lift meat loaf out of pan, allowing excess juices to drip into pan. Transfer to warmed serving plate; remove foil. Skim off fat; spoon pan juices over top, if desired. Makes 6 servings.

Meat loaf jokes will grind to a halt when your family sits down to this moist reputation-making version. Go the Mom route and serve with mashed potatoes, even peas and carrots if you like. One tasty update you shouldn't miss is caramelized onions atop the potatoes — fry sliced onions slowly in very little oil or butter until golden and spoon tender.

Oven-Baked Curried Chicken Legs

4	chicken legs	4
1 tbsp	curry powder	15 mL
1 tsp	vegetable oil	5 mL
1/3 cup	plain yogurt	75 mL
2 tbsp	lemon juice	25 mL
1 tsp	packed brown sugar	5 mL

● Trim off any fat and excess skin from chicken; cut at joint into thighs and drumsticks.

● In small saucepan, heat curry powder and oil over medium heat, stirring often, for 3 minutes or until bubbling; pour into large bowl. Whisk in yogurt, lemon juice and sugar. Add chicken, turning to coat; marinate at room temperature for 30 minutes.

● Place chicken, fleshy side up, on foil-lined baking sheet; brush with remaining marinade. Bake in 425°F (220°C) oven for 35 to 40 minutes or until browned and juices run clear when chicken is pierced. Makes 4 servings.

A yogurt and curry marinade keeps affordable chicken legs tender and moist. Serve with rice, sliced bananas tossed with lemon juice and a cucumber and radish salad tossed with yogurt, chopped fresh mint and a touch of cayenne.

Sesame Chicken ▲

Lots of sesame seeds add crunch to baked chicken. Dark sesame oil, extracted from roasted seeds, picks up on the flavor.

4	chicken legs	4
1/4 cup	oyster sauce	50 mL
4 tsp	liquid honey	20 mL
2 tsp	Dijon mustard	10 mL
1/2 tsp	sesame oil	2 mL
Pinch	pepper	Pinch
2 tbsp	sesame seeds	25 mL
1	green onion, chopped	1

● Remove skin from chicken and discard. If desired, cut at joint into thighs and drumsticks. Arrange on greased baking sheet.

● Combine oyster sauce, honey, mustard, sesame oil and pepper; brush over chicken. Sprinkle with sesame seeds.

● Bake in 375°F (190°C) oven for 40 minutes or until juices run clear when chicken is pierced. Serve sprinkled with onion. Makes 4 servings.

Cardamom Chicken

4	boneless skinless chicken breasts	4
1 tsp	vegetable oil	5 mL
2	onions, sliced	2
2 tsp	each ground cardamom and coriander	10 mL
1 tsp	turmeric	5 mL
1 tsp	chili powder	5 mL
1	can (19 oz/540 mL) tomatoes	1
1/2 cup	water	125 mL
1-1/2 tsp	cornstarch	7 mL
1/2 cup	plain yogurt	125 mL

● Cut chicken into 1-1/2-inch (4 cm) cubes. In deep skillet, heat oil over medium-high heat; cook chicken for about 5 minutes or until browned. Remove chicken and set aside.

● Reduce heat to medium-low; add onions, cardamom, coriander, turmeric and chili powder; cook, stirring, for 3 minutes or until onions are softened.

● Add tomatoes, breaking up with fork. Return chicken to pan; add water and bring to simmer. Cook, stirring occasionally, for about 30 minutes or until chicken is no longer pink inside.

● Remove 1/2 cup (125 mL) of the sauce to small bowl; whisk in 1 tsp (5 mL) of the cornstarch. Stir cornstarch mixture back into pan and bring to boil; cook, stirring, for 1 to 2 minutes or until thickened. Stir remaining cornstarch into yogurt; stir into sauce and heat through but do not boil. Makes 4 servings.

This one-dish meal almost cooks itself and is a flavorful introduction to the very aromatic spice — cardamom. Mango chutney goes well with it, as does basmati rice.

Tangy Chicken Livers

1-1/2 lb	chicken livers	750 g
1 tbsp	vegetable oil	15 mL
1	onion, chopped	1
2 tbsp	balsamic or red wine vinegar	25 mL
1 tsp	crumbled dried sage	5 mL
1/4 tsp	each salt and pepper	1 mL
2 tbsp	chopped fresh parsley	25 mL

● Trim any fat and connective tissue from livers. In large skillet, heat oil over medium-high heat; cook livers, turning often, for 2 minutes. Add onion; cook, stirring occasionally, for 2 minutes.

● Add vinegar, sage, salt and pepper; cook, stirring often, for 5 minutes or until livers are tender and still slightly pink inside. With slotted spoon, remove livers to heated platter.

● Add 1/2 cup (125 mL) water to pan; boil for 1 minute, stirring to scrape up brown bits. Pour over livers. Garnish with parsley. Makes 4 servings.

This is no ordinary skilletful of chicken livers to be eaten out of a sense of economic or nutritional duty. A splash of balsamic vinegar and a crumble of sage enliven the liver's gentle flavor. Serve with baked sweet potatoes and a spinach salad.

Salmon Patties

An easy lemon sauce turns old-time salmon patties into something deliciously different. Serve as a burger in a toasted bun, or sidle some new potatoes and a green salad alongside.

2	cans (each 7-1/2 oz/213 g) sockeye salmon, drained	2
1	small onion, chopped	1
1/2 cup	dry bread crumbs	125 mL
1	egg, lightly beaten	1
1/4 tsp	pepper	1 mL
1/4 tsp	dried dillweed	1 mL
1/2 tsp	vegetable oil	2 mL
	LEMON MAYO	
1/4 cup	light mayonnaise	50 mL
1 tbsp	lemon juice	15 mL
2 tsp	capers or diced dill pickle	10 mL

● In bowl, mash salmon and bones with fork; mix in onion, 2 tbsp (25 mL) of the bread crumbs, egg, pepper and dill. Shape into eight 1/2-inch (1 cm) thick patties. Spread remaining crumbs on plate; press patties into crumbs to coat both sides.

● In nonstick skillet, heat oil over medium heat; cook patties, turning once, for about 8 minutes or until crisp and golden.

● LEMON MAYO: In bowl, stir together mayonnaise, lemon juice and capers. Serve with patties. Makes 4 servings.

TIP: Be sure to leave the bones in canned salmon. They add calcium to the diet and are never noticed in the finished dish.

Shrimp Fried Rice

When cooking rice for one meal, why not cook enough for leftovers and this easy fried rice supper? If shrimp isn't a go in your household, substitute chopped leftover barbecued fish, chicken or pork, or simply leave it out. (see Cooking Rice, p. 8)

1 tbsp	vegetable oil	15 mL
1	egg, beaten	1
1	small onion, thinly sliced	1
1	clove garlic, chopped	1
1	small carrot, grated	1
1	stalk celery, chopped	1
1/2 cup	sliced mushrooms	125 mL
4 cups	cooled cooked rice	1 L
1/3 cup	each frozen peas and corn kernels	75 mL
1/2 cup	cooked baby shrimp	125 mL
3 tbsp	soy sauce	50 mL

● In wok or large nonstick skillet, heat 1 tsp (5 mL) of the oil over medium heat; cook egg, stirring, until scrambled and set. Remove from pan and let cool; cut into 1-inch (2.5 cm) pieces and set aside.

● Wipe out pan and heat remaining oil over medium-high heat; cook onion and garlic, stirring, for 3 minutes or until starting to brown. Add carrot, celery and mushrooms; cook for about 5 minutes or until mushrooms are golden.

● Break up any lumps of rice and add to pan along with peas, corn, shrimp, soy sauce and 2 tbsp (25 mL) water; cover and cook, stirring once, for 3 to 4 minutes or until hot. Gently stir in reserved egg. Makes 6 servings.

Salmon and Potato Strata ▲

1	can (7-1/2 oz/213 g) red sockeye salmon	1
2	stalks celery, sliced	2
1	onion, chopped	1
4	eggs, lightly beaten	4
1-1/3 cups	milk	325 mL
3/4 tsp	each paprika and salt	4 mL
1/2 tsp	each pepper and dried tarragon	2 mL
4	potatoes, peeled and thinly sliced	4
1/2 cup	dry bread crumbs	125 mL
1/4 cup	chopped fresh parsley	50 mL
2 tbsp	butter, cut into bits	25 mL

● In large bowl, mash salmon, juices and bones with fork; stir in celery, onion, eggs, milk, paprika, 1/2 tsp (2 mL) of the salt, pepper and tarragon until well mixed.

● In greased 8-cup (2 L) casserole, arrange half of the potatoes over bottom of dish; sprinkle with remaining salt. Pour salmon mixture over top; layer remaining potatoes over top.

● Combine bread crumbs and parsley; sprinkle over potatoes. Dot with butter. Bake in 350°F (180°C) oven for 75 minutes or until potatoes are tender. Makes 4 servings.

Layered potato slices and salmon make up this unapologetically homey and economical main dish so suited to cool weather. Serve with green peas or beans and pass a bowl of salsa or chili sauce.

Baked Italian Fish

A *thyme-infused tomato topping is extra insurance that the fish will turn out moist and delicious.*

1-1/2 lb	cod, haddock or bluefish fillets	750 g
1 tbsp	lemon juice	15 mL
1	green onion, chopped	1
1 tsp	dried thyme	5 mL
1/4 tsp	(approx) each salt and pepper	1 mL
1	can (14 oz/398 mL) tomatoes, drained and chopped	1
1 cup	shredded Cheddar or Monterey Jack cheese	250 mL

● In greased casserole, arrange fillets in single layer, folding thin ends under for equal thickness. Drizzle with lemon juice; sprinkle with onion, 1/2 tsp (2 mL) of the thyme, salt and pepper.

● Combine tomatoes with remaining thyme; season with more salt and pepper to taste. Spoon over fish.

● Bake in 450°F (230°C) oven for 10 minutes. Sprinkle with Cheddar; bake for 2 to 3 minutes or until Cheddar has melted and fish flakes easily when tested with fork. Makes 4 servings.

TIP: When planning a menu that includes baking one dish in the oven, always try to cook something else in the oven, too. If you choose roasted potatoes, sweet potatoes, onions or squash as vegetables, be sure to start them off first. Ditto baked rice.

Almond Trout

D *elicate salmon-pink trout fillets splashed with lemon and strewn with golden toasted almonds are so fast and easy you'll want to serve them year -round.*

2 tbsp	butter	25 mL
1/2 cup	sliced almonds	125 mL
1-1/2 lb	trout fillets	750 g
2 tbsp	lemon juice	25 mL
1/4 tsp	pepper	1 mL
1/4 cup	finely chopped green onions	50 mL

● In large nonstick skillet, heat butter over medium-high heat until browned and sizzling stops. Stir in almonds; cook, stirring, for 1 to 2 minutes or until golden. With slotted spoon, remove almonds and set aside.

● Add fillets, skin side up; cook for 4 to 5 minutes or just until edges are opaque and bottom is browned. Turn and cook for 2 minutes. Sprinkle with lemon juice and pepper; cook for 1 to 2 minutes or until fish flakes easily when tested with fork. With slotted spatula, remove fillets to heated serving platter.

● Return almonds to pan; stir in green onions. Pour over fish. Makes 4 servings.

Asparagus Pasta Toss

Creamy without cream — that's how to describe this fast-and-easy weeknight supper. Lemon contributes a sparkling freshness.

TIP: Evaporated milk works like cream in a pasta sauce — coating the vegetables and pasta, and giving a lush, rich taste with a minimum of fat.

2 lb	asparagus, trimmed	1 kg
1 cup	sliced sweet red pepper	250 mL
1 tbsp	olive oil	15 mL
3 cups	sliced mushrooms	750 mL
1	onion, chopped	1
1	clove garlic, minced	1
1 tsp	dried tarragon	5 mL
2 tbsp	all-purpose flour	25 mL
1	can (385 mL) 2% evaporated milk	1
1 tsp	grated lemon rind	5 mL
2 tbsp	lemon juice	25 mL
1 tsp	salt	5 mL
1/4 tsp	pepper	1 mL
4 cups	penne	1 L

● Cut asparagus into 2-1/2-inch (6 cm) pieces. In pot of boiling water, cook asparagus for 2 minutes; add red pepper and cook for 1 minute. Drain and set vegetables aside.

● In same pot, heat oil over medium heat; cook mushrooms, onion, garlic and tarragon, covered and stirring occasionally, for 3 minutes. Sprinkle with flour; stir until smooth. Gradually whisk in milk; cook, stirring, for 4 minutes or until thickened. Stir in lemon rind and juice, salt and pepper.

● Meanwhile, in large pot of boiling salted water, cook penne for 8 to 10 minutes or until tender but firm; drain and return to pot. Add sauce and asparagus mixture; cook, stirring, over low heat until heated through. Makes 4 servings.

Lazy Lasagna Toss

For everyone who loves lasagna but doesn't always have the time it takes to make it, here's an easy way to get all the great flavors of lasagna — zesty sausage, tomato sauce, pasta and a dollop of creamy ricotta — in a no-bake, no-layer, no-fuss toss.

1 lb	hot Italian sausages	500 g
1 tsp	vegetable oil	5 mL
3 cups	chunky vegetable spaghetti sauce	750 mL
1 cup	ricotta cheese	250 mL
1/4 cup	freshly grated Parmesan cheese	50 mL
2 tbsp	finely chopped fresh parsley	25 mL
4 cups	pasta shells or fusilli	1 L

● Remove sausages from casings. In large skillet, heat oil over medium-high heat; cook sausage, stirring and breaking up with fork, for 5 to 6 minutes or until no longer pink. Drain off fat. Stir in spaghetti sauce; cook for 3 to 4 minutes or until bubbly.

● Meanwhile, in small microwaveable bowl or in saucepan, mix ricotta with Parmesan; microwave at High for 45 seconds, or cook over medium heat for 3 minutes, or just until Parmesan begins to melt. Stir in parsley.

● Meanwhile, in large pot of boiling salted water, cook pasta for 8 to 10 minutes or until tender but firm; drain well and toss with spaghetti sauce. Divide among bowls; spoon ricotta mixture evenly over top. Makes 4 servings.

RICOTTA CHEESE

This creamy rich-tasting fresh cheese is made from the whey drained off during the making of mozzarella cheese. You'll find it in tubs in the dairy case of grocery stores and supermarkets — in both regular and low-fat versions. Like cottage cheese, it is slightly grainy but can be smoothed by whizzing in a food processor or blender. It has a sweet dairy taste and fairly firm consistency, making it especially suitable as a stuffing and for pasta dishes and desserts alike.

Creamy Broccoli Pasta ▼

12 oz	linguine or spaghetti	375 g
3 cups	coarsely chopped broccoli florets	750 mL
1-1/2 cups	chicken or vegetable stock	375 mL
1 tsp	all-purpose flour	5 mL
1	pkg (250 g) light herb cream cheese	250 mL
	Salt and pepper	
	freshly grated Parmesan cheese (optional)	

● In large pot of boiling salted water, cook linguine for 6 minutes. Add broccoli; cook for 2 minutes or until linguine is tender but firm and broccoli is tender-crisp. Drain and return to pot.

● Meanwhile, in small saucepan, heat chicken stock over medium-high heat; whisk in flour and cook, stirring, for 3 to 5 minutes or until slightly thickened.

● Remove from heat; whisk in cream cheese until melted. Toss with pasta mixture. Season with salt and pepper to taste. Sprinkle with Parmesan (if using). Makes 4 servings.

B*y the time the water for the pasta boils, the light herbed cream sauce is ready. Then, it's only minutes until this broccoli-flecked dish is on the table. Add a leafy lettuce, red onion and sliced mushroom salad. For the photograph, we used a new pasta called "I Tegolacci."*

(clockwise from left) Warm Caesar Salad Pasta (p. 33), Roasted Tomato Penne, Pesto Chicken Pasta Salad (p. 55)

Roasted Tomato Penne ▲

Roasted tomatoes, bursting with sunny summer flavor, marry beautifully with garlic and basil in a superlative pasta dish that will win hearty accolades each time you serve it.

12	large plum tomatoes	12
10	large cloves garlic	10
1 cup	packed fresh basil leaves	250 mL
1/2 tsp	salt	2 mL
1/4 tsp	pepper	1 mL
1/3 cup	extra virgin olive oil	75 mL
4 cups	penne or rotini	1 L
1 cup	crumbled feta cheese	250 mL

● Slice tomatoes in half lengthwise; place, cut side up, in greased shallow roasting pan.

● In food processor, coarsely chop together garlic, basil, salt and pepper; with motor running, gradually pour in oil. Spread over cut sides of tomatoes.

● Bake in 350°F (180°C) oven for 2 hours or until withered and edges are browned. Chop into 1/2-inch (1 cm) pieces.

● Meanwhile, in large pot of boiling salted water, cook penne for 8 to 10 minutes or until tender but firm; drain and return to pot. Toss with most of the tomatoes. Serve sprinkled with feta and remaining tomatoes. Makes 4 servings.

Warm Caesar Salad Pasta ◄

1/2 cup	extra virgin olive oil	125 mL
4	slices (1/2 inch/1 cm thick) Italian bread	4
3/4 tsp	each salt and pepper	4 mL
1/4 tsp	grated lemon rind	1 mL
1/4 cup	lemon juice	50 mL
3	cloves garlic, minced	3
6	anchovy fillets	6
1/3 cup	freshly grated Parmesan cheese	75 mL
4 cups	penne	1 L
6	slices bacon, cooked and crumbled	6
4 cups	coarsely shredded romaine lettuce	1 L

● Brush 2 tbsp (25 mL) of the oil over both sides of bread. Cut into 1/2-inch (1 cm) cubes; toss with 1/4 tsp (1 mL) each of the salt and pepper. Toast on baking sheet in 350°F (180°C) oven for 10 minutes or until golden and crisp. Set croutons aside.

● In food processor, purée together lemon rind and juice, garlic, anchovies and remaining salt and pepper. With motor running, gradually pour in remaining oil. Blend in half of the Parmesan.

● Meanwhile, in large pot of boiling salted water, cook penne for 8 to 10 minutes or until tender but firm. Reserving 1/4 cup (50 mL) cooking water, drain penne and return to pot over low heat.

● Toss with garlic mixture and enough of the cooking liquid to moisten. Toss with croutons, bacon and lettuce. Serve sprinkled with remaining Parmesan. Makes 6 servings.

C*runchy with croutons, smoky with bacon, and (dare it be said?) loaded with garlic, Caesar salad fixings are a fine toss with pasta and greens.*

TIP: Anchovy paste is a convenient alternative to anchovy fillets. If substituting in this recipe, use 2 tsp (10 mL) and store tube in refrigerator.

Shell Pasta with Vegetables and Clams

1	can (142 g) baby clams	1
2 tbsp	vegetable oil	25 mL
1	onion, chopped	1
2	each carrots and stalks celery, chopped	2
2	cloves garlic, minced	2
Pinch	hot pepper flakes	Pinch
1	can (28 oz/796 mL) tomatoes	1
1 tsp	dried basil	5 mL
2	zucchini, chopped	2
1 tsp	lemon juice	5 mL
	Salt and pepper	
6 cups	large shell pasta	1.5 L

● Drain clams, reserving juice and clams separately; set aside.

● In saucepan, heat oil over medium-high heat; cook onion, carrots, celery, garlic and hot pepper flakes, stirring, for 3 minutes. Stir in tomatoes, breaking up with spoon.

● Add clam juice and basil; bring to boil. Reduce heat to medium-low; cook, stirring occasionally, for 20 minutes. Add zucchini; cook for 10 to 15 minutes or until sauce is thickened. Stir in clams; season with lemon juice, and salt and pepper to taste.

● Meanwhile, in large pot of boiling salted water, cook pasta for 8 to 10 minutes or until tender but firm; drain and return to pot. Add sauce and toss gently to coat. Makes 4 servings.

K*eep a few cans of baby clams and tomatoes on hand for this no-fail seafood pasta.*

Chili Salad with Lots of Vegetables

Lean ground beef and a wealth of vegetables add up to a one-dish meal that's both fast and nutritious. Serve with light and crispy taco chips you can make at home (see box, below).

1 lb	lean ground beef	500 g
1	onion, chopped	1
1	clove garlic, minced	1
1	sweet green pepper, chopped	1
3	tomatoes, chopped	3
1 tbsp	chili powder	15 mL
1 tsp	each cinnamon and salt	5 mL
1/2 tsp	each oregano and ground cumin	2 mL
1/4 tsp	hot pepper sauce	1 mL
8 cups	shredded iceberg lettuce	2 L
3	green onions, chopped	3
1 cup	shredded Cheddar cheese	250 mL
1/4 cup	plain yogurt	50 mL

● In large nonstick skillet, cook beef, breaking up with fork, for 4 minutes or until no longer pink; drain off fat. Add onion, garlic and half of the green pepper; cook for 4 minutes or until softened.

● Stir in two-thirds of the tomatoes, the chili powder, cinnamon, salt, oregano, cumin and hot pepper sauce; cook, stirring often, for 5 minutes or until most of the liquid has evaporated.

● Arrange lettuce on platter or individual plates; spoon beef mixture over top. Sprinkle green onions, remaining green pepper and tomato, then Cheddar over beef mixture. Serve with yogurt. Makes 4 servings.

TIP: Light-style Cheddar is a lower-fat alternative (42 calories and 3 g fat for 2 tbsp/25 mL) to regular Cheddar (57 calories and 5 g fat) for the same amount.

LIGHT BAKED TACO CHIPS
● Brush both sides of 6 flour tortillas lightly with 1 tbsp (15 mL) vegetable oil; sprinkle with salt and chili powder, if desired. Cut each tortilla into 8 wedges.
● Bake on baking sheet in 350°F (180°C) oven for 15 minutes; turn and bake for 5 minutes or until crisp. Makes 4 servings.

Spicy Noodle Salad

A bass note of orange highlights this melody of Asian flavors, crunchy textures and cool silky pasta. (Photo, p. 4)

12 oz	spaghetti	375 g
2 tbsp	sesame oil	25 mL
1-1/2 cups	grated carrots	375 mL
1-1/2 cups	bean sprouts	375 mL
4	green onions, chopped	4
1 tbsp	grated orange rind	15 mL
1/4 cup	orange juice	50 mL
1/4 cup	tahini (optional)	50 mL
3 tbsp	soy sauce	50 mL
1 tsp	granulated sugar	5 mL
1 tsp	hot pepper sauce	5 mL
1/2 cup	chopped peanuts	125 mL
1/4 cup	chopped fresh coriander	50 mL

● In large pot of boiling salted water, cook spaghetti for 8 to 10 minutes or until tender but firm; drain and rinse under cold water. Drain well and transfer to bowl.

● Add sesame oil to spaghetti; toss to coat. Add carrots, bean sprouts, onions and orange rind.

● Combine orange juice, tahini (if using), soy sauce, sugar and hot pepper sauce; toss with spaghetti mixture. Sprinkle with peanuts and coriander. Makes 4 servings.

Healthy Processor Pizza Crust

1 cup	whole wheat flour	250 mL
1-1/2 cups	(approx) all-purpose flour	375 mL
1	pkg quick-rising (instant) dry yeast (or 1 tbsp/15 mL)	1
1 tsp	salt	5 mL
1/2 tsp	granulated sugar	2 mL
2 tsp	olive oil	10 mL

● In food processor, combine whole wheat flour, 1 cup (250 mL) of the all-purpose flour, yeast, salt and sugar. With motor running, gradually pour in oil and 3/4 cup (175 mL) very hot water (125°F/50°C), beating and adding up to 1/4 cup (50 mL) more water if necessary to form dough into ball. Process for 1 minute.

● Turn out dough onto lightly floured surface. Knead for 5 minutes or until smooth and elastic, adding more flour if necessary. Cover and let rest for 10 minutes. *(Dough can be refrigerated for up to 2 days.)* On lightly floured surface, roll out dough into 12-inch (30 cm) circle. Makes 1 unbaked pizza crust.

Whole wheat flour ups the B vitamins in this quick pizza base. The dough can be refrigerated overnight, ready to roll and bake the next day.

Friday Night Family Pizza ▼

1	Healthy Processor Pizza Crust (recipe, this page)	1
1/4 cup	water	50 mL
2 tbsp	tomato paste	25 mL
3/4 tsp	dried oregano	4 mL
1	sweet green pepper, cut into strips	1
1/2 cup	sliced mushrooms	125 mL
Half	small onion, thinly sliced	Half
1-1/2 cups	shredded mozzarella cheese	375 mL

● Place pizza crust on perforated pizza pan or baking sheet. Combine water, tomato paste and oregano; spread over crust.

● Arrange green pepper, mushrooms and onion over top; sprinkle with mozzarella. Bake in 500°F (260°C) oven for 12 to 15 minutes or until crust is crisp. Makes 4 servings.

Canadian Living's nutrition editor, Anne Lindsay, proposes this homemade lightened-up version of take-out pizza for those Friday nights when only a pizza and video will do. Top with some shaved ham or thinly sliced low-fat deli meats to give a pepperoni-style punch without all the fat.

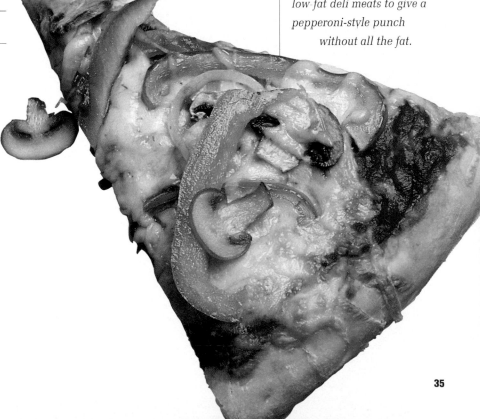

Cheesy Sloppy Joe Pizza

*We think this kid-pleaser
of a sauce is even better on a
prebaked pizza crust than it
ever was on a bun. While the
pizza bakes, toss a leafy
greens and cucumber salad
with a dilly ranch dressing.*

1 tsp	vegetable oil	5 mL
12 oz	lean ground beef	375 g
3/4 cup	spicy spaghetti sauce	175 mL
1 cup	corn kernels	250 mL
1/2 tsp	salt	2 mL
1/4 tsp	pepper	1 mL
1	(10-inch/25 cm) prebaked pizza crust	1
1/2 cup	chopped green onions	125 mL
1 cup	shredded Monterey Jack cheese	250 mL

● In large skillet, heat oil over medium heat; cook beef, breaking up with back of spoon, for 4 to 5 minutes or until no longer pink. Drain off fat. Stir in spaghetti sauce, corn, salt and pepper.

● Place pizza crust on perforated pizza pan or baking sheet; spread sauce over crust. Sprinkle with onions; scatter cheese over top. Bake in 400°F (200°C) oven for 20 to 25 minutes or until cheese is bubbly and golden. Makes 4 servings.

Smiley Freezer Pizza ▼

*When there are busy days
ahead, get ready with a pizza
or two tucked in the freezer.
Making your own crust is an
affordable way to enjoy pizza
more often, but ready-made
chilled pizza dough or
prebaked pizza crusts are
perfectly good alternatives.*

1	(12-inch/30 cm) prebaked pizza crust	1
1 cup	chunky vegetable spaghetti sauce	250 mL
1 cup	shredded mozzarella cheese	250 mL
1/4 cup	freshly grated Parmesan cheese	50 mL

2 oz	sliced ham	50 g
Half	sweet green and/or red pepper	Half
1/3 cup	frozen green peas	75 mL

● Spread pizza crust with spaghetti sauce; sprinkle with mozzarella and Parmesan.

● Cut ham and sweet pepper into shapes for eyes and mouth. Arrange over cheese along with peas to make faces. Wrap and freeze pizza for up to 1 week.

● Place frozen pizza on perforated pizza pan or baking sheet. Bake on bottom rack in 425°F (220°C) oven for about 15 minutes or until golden. Let stand for 5 minutes. Makes 4 servings.

Onion and Potato Pizza

2	potatoes	2
2 tbsp	olive oil	25 mL
2	cloves garlic, minced	2
1	red onion, sliced	1
2 tsp	crumbled dried rosemary	10 mL
1	Healthy Processor Pizza Crust (recipe, p. 35)	1
3 tbsp	freshly grated Parmesan cheese	50 mL
Pinch	each salt and pepper	Pinch

● Peel potatoes. In pot of boiling salted water, cook potatoes for 10 minutes or until almost tender but still firm; drain well and slice thinly. Set aside.

● Meanwhile, in skillet, heat oil over medium heat; cook garlic, onion and rosemary, stirring occasionally, for 15 minutes or until golden.

● Place pizza crust on perforated pizza pan or baking sheet; sprinkle with 1 tbsp (15 mL) of the Parmesan. Arrange potatoes over top, overlapping slightly; top with onion mixture. Season with salt and pepper; sprinkle with remaining Parmesan.

● Bake in 500°F (260°C) oven for 12 to 15 minutes or until crust is crisp. Makes 4 servings.

Believe it or not, golden onions and potatoes are sensational as a pizza topping!

Snacking Pizza

1	Healthy Processor Pizza Crust (recipe, p. 35)	1
3/4 cup	chunky-style salsa	175 mL
1 cup	shredded Cheddar cheese	250 mL

● Place pizza crust on perforated pizza pan or baking sheet. Spread with salsa, leaving 1-inch (2.5 cm) border; sprinkle with Cheddar. Bake in 500°F (260°C) oven for 12 to 15 minutes or until crust is crisp. Makes 4 servings.

A superfast pizza is even faster with a prebaked crust and store-bought salsa. Toss up a salad while the pizza crisps.

Veggie-Stuffed Baked Potato for One

1	baking potato	1
1/4 cup	each shredded Cheddar and freshly grated Parmesan cheese	50 mL
1/4 cup	diced sweet green pepper	50 mL
1/4 cup	coarsely chopped mushrooms	50 mL
Pinch	dried oregano or Italian seasoning	Pinch
Half	tomato, diced	Half
2 tbsp	plain yogurt	25 mL
Pinch	each salt and pepper	Pinch

● Scrub potato and prick in several places with fork. Place on paper towel; microwave at High for 6 to 7 minutes or until tender. (Or, bake in 400°F/200°C toaster oven for 1 hour.)

● Reserve 2 tbsp (25 mL) of the Cheddar. In bowl, combine remaining Cheddar, Parmesan, green pepper, mushrooms, oregano and tomato.

● Cut cooked potato in half and scoop out pulp to bowl; mash pulp with yogurt. Stir into cheese mixture.

● Mound potato mixture into potato shells. Microwave at High for 3 to 4 minutes or until heated through. (Or, bake in 400°F/200°C toaster oven for 15 to 20 minutes.) Sprinkle with salt, pepper and reserved Cheddar. Makes 1 serving.

Raid the crisper and you'll find most of the ingredients you need for this satisfying supper. When company comes, simply multiply the ingredients.

Touch of Thai Seafood Soup ▲

Surprise the family with a quick and satisfying soup that's chock-full of noodles, delicious scallops and thinly sliced vegetables — because even weeknight suppers deserve a splurge now and then!

1-1/2 lb	fresh scallops	750 g
2 tsp	sesame oil	10 mL
3	cloves garlic, minced	3
6 cups	chicken stock	1.5 L
1/4 tsp	fennel seeds	1 mL
3 cups	frozen stir-fry or Japanese-style vegetables	750 mL
6 oz	capellini	175 g
1 tbsp	finely slivered gingerroot	15 mL
1/4 cup	fresh coriander or parsley leaves	50 mL
	Pepper	

● Remove connective muscle from scallops; cut scallops into bite-size pieces. Set aside.

● In Dutch oven, heat oil over medium heat; cook garlic, stirring, for 1 minute. Add stock and fennel seeds; bring to simmer. Add vegetables; bring to boil.

● Stir in capellini and ginger; cover, reduce heat and simmer for 3 minutes or until pasta is almost tender but firm.

● Add coriander and scallops; simmer for 2 minutes or until scallops are opaque. Season with pepper to taste. Makes 6 servings.

Lightly Spiced Squash Gumbo

1	buttercup squash (about 1-1/2 lb/750 g)	1
1 tsp	vegetable oil	5 mL
1/2 tsp	each cinnamon and ground cumin	2 mL
1	large onion, chopped	1
1	can (19 oz/540 mL) tomatoes, puréed	1
1 cup	vegetable stock	250 mL
1 tbsp	chopped fresh or drained bottled red peppers	15 mL
16	frozen okra pods, chopped (or 1-1/2 cups/375 mL green peas)	16
1	can (19 oz/540 mL) chick-peas, drained and rinsed	1
	Pepper	

● Peel and seed squash; cut into thick wedges and set aside.

● In Dutch oven or heavy saucepan, heat oil over medium heat; stir in cinnamon and cumin for about 1 minute or until fragrant. Add onion; cook, stirring occasionally, for 5 minutes or until softened.

● Add tomatoes, stock, red peppers and squash; bring to simmer. Cook over medium heat for 10 to 12 minutes or until squash is tender but still slightly firm.

● Add okra and chick-peas; cover and cook for about 6 minutes or until squash is just tender. Season with pepper to taste. Makes 6 servings.

This vegetarian stew takes very little time to prepare and makes an ideal weeknight supper. It's especially tasty spooned over couscous.

Tortellini Soup with Peas

3	cloves garlic, minced	3
1/2 lb	frozen cheese tortellini	250 g
1	can (10 oz/284 mL) chicken broth	1
1 cup	frozen peas	250 mL
1/4 tsp	pepper	1 mL
1/4 cup	freshly grated Parmesan cheese	50 mL

● In large pot, bring 3 cups (750 mL) water and garlic to boil. Add frozen tortellini; return to boil. Reduce heat to medium-high; cook, stirring occasionally, for 15 minutes.

● Add chicken broth, 1-1/4 cups (300 mL) water and peas; return to boil. Reduce heat to medium; cook for 5 minutes or until pasta is tender but firm. Stir in pepper. Serve sprinkled with Parmesan. Makes 3 servings.

When time is really short, convenient ingredients such as tortellini and cans of chicken broth let you put a hearty meal on the table in no time at all.

MEASURING LIQUIDS

Measuring correctly is essential to successful cooking. It starts with using the right utensils.

● Liquid measuring cups (or measures, as they are called in the metric system) are used only for liquids. These cups are usually glass, with amounts from 1 cup (250 mL) to 8 cups (2 L) clearly marked on the side, and with a space between the amount and the rim to prevent spills. A spout facilitates pouring. These measures make excellent containers for microwave cooking.

● To measure liquids, place cup on level work surface. Fill to required amount. To read the amount accurately, read at eye level.

Easy Entertaining

What's more important? Family and friends or fussing?
The first, of course — and when the cooking is this relaxed and easy,
getting together becomes the pleasure it should be.

White Bean Spread and Pita Crisps ▶

*This easy appetizer is sure
to win raves from your guests.
Serve with vegetables, or rice
or water crackers, in addition
to the pita triangles.*

1/3 cup	olive oil	75 mL
3	large cloves garlic, minced	3
3/4 tsp	ground coriander	4 mL
1/2 tsp	each salt and pepper	2 mL
3	pita breads	3
1	can (19 oz/540 mL) white kidney beans, drained and rinsed	1
1/4 cup	lemon juice	50 mL
1 tbsp	tahini	15 mL
1/2 tsp	ground cumin	2 mL
1/2 tsp	hot pepper sauce	2 mL
3 tbsp	chopped fresh coriander	50 mL

● Stir together 2 tbsp (25 mL) of the olive oil, one-third of the garlic, 1/4 tsp (1 mL) of the ground coriander and pinch each of the salt and pepper.

● Cut pitas into 6 rounds; cut into triangles and place on baking sheet. Brush triangles with olive oil mixture. Bake in 350°F (180°C) oven for 8 to 10 minutes or until crisp.

● Meanwhile, in food processor, purée together remaining olive oil, garlic, ground coriander, salt and pepper, kidney beans, lemon juice, tahini, cumin and hot pepper sauce. Stir in fresh coriander. *(Spread can be refrigerated in airtight container for up to 2 days.)* Serve with pita crisps. Makes 2 cups (500 mL).

TIP: Tahini is a thick paste of ground sesame seeds available at Middle Eastern and specialty food stores. Many supermarkets sell it in the section with Kosher ingredients.

Herbed Quark Spread

*Low-fat quark is the basis
for a fresh spread that's
ideal on melba rounds or for
stuffing into celery.*

1 cup	quark cheese	250 mL
1/4 cup	chopped fresh basil (or 1/2 tsp/2 mL dried)	50 mL
1	green onion, chopped	1
1	clove garlic, minced	1
Dash	hot pepper sauce	Dash
	Salt and pepper	

● In small bowl, combine quark, basil, onion, garlic, hot pepper sauce, and salt and pepper to taste. *(Spread can be covered and refrigerated for up to 8 hours; stir before serving.)* Makes 1 cup (250 mL).

Roasted Pepper and Tomato Spread ▼

Here's an idea for quick summer appetizers. Spread this vibrantly red and robust Mediterranean purée over split mini pita breads, sprinkle with crumbled feta and slivered olives, then broil. It's also delicious in sandwiches and over burgers, especially chicken.

3	sweet red peppers	3
4	cloves garlic	4
2 tbsp	olive oil	25 mL
1/2 cup	tomato paste	125 mL
1 tbsp	butter	15 mL
Pinch	cayenne pepper	Pinch
	Salt	

● Broil or grill red peppers, turning several times, for about 20 minutes or until blistered and charred. Let cool slightly; peel, seed and cut into chunks.

● In 8-inch (2 L) square baking dish, toss together peppers, garlic and oil; bake in 300°F (150°C) oven, stirring occasionally, for 1 hour or until garlic is very soft. Stir in tomato paste; bake for 15 to 20 minutes or until surface appears dry.

● In food processor or blender, purée pepper mixture, butter and cayenne until smooth. Season with salt to taste. *(Spread can be refrigerated in airtight container for up to 2 weeks or frozen for up to 2 months.)* Makes about 1 cup (250 mL).

(top) Roasted Pepper and Tomato Spread; (bottom) Peppered Yogurt Cheese (p. 43)

Spanish Omelette Tapas

2 tbsp	olive oil	25 mL
3 cups	diced peeled potatoes	750 mL
3 cups	chopped onions	750 mL
1 tsp	salt	5 mL
1/4 tsp	dried marjoram	1 mL
	Pepper	
10	eggs	10
2 tbsp	chopped fresh parsley	25 mL
	Paprika	

● In large skillet, heat oil over medium-low heat; stir in potatoes, onions, 3/4 tsp (4 mL) of the salt, marjoram, and pepper to taste. Cover and cook, stirring frequently and without browning, for 10 to 15 minutes or until potato is tender. Spread in greased 13- x 9-inch (3 L) baking dish.

● Whisk together eggs, parsley, remaining salt and pinch of pepper; pour over potato mixture, making sure egg mixture flows to bottom of dish.

● Bake in 350°F (180°C) oven for about 20 minutes or until set. Let cool on rack. *(Omelette can be covered and refrigerated for up to 1 day; bring to room temperature.)* Sprinkle with paprika to taste; cut into squares. Makes 48 appetizers.

A classic from Spain, this thick potato omelette is an inexpensive and very pleasing appetizer to serve warm or at room temperature. Let guests help themselves with toothpicks.

Tuna Melt Pitas

1	can (7 oz/184 g) flaked white tuna	1
3/4 cup	diced celery	175 mL
3/4 cup	shredded Cheddar cheese	175 mL
1/3 cup	mayonnaise	75 mL
2	green onions, chopped	2
2 tbsp	green pickle relish	25 mL
10	mini pita breads	10
	Paprika	

● Drain and flake tuna. In bowl, combine tuna, celery, Cheddar, mayonnaise, onions and relish.

● Cut pitas in half to form circles; arrange on baking sheet. Top each half with heaping tablespoon (15 mL) tuna mixture. Sprinkle with paprika to taste. *(Pitas can be prepared to this point, covered and refrigerated for up to 1 day.)*

● Bake in 350°F (180°C) oven for 15 minutes or until Cheddar melts. Makes 20 appetizers.

A favorite with kids and adults alike, these tasty appetizers can be made ahead and baked at the last moment.

PEPPERED YOGURT CHEESE

Flavored with green peppercorns and thyme, this creamy spread is delicious lavished over thick cucumber slices or melba toast. (photo, p. 42)

● In double-thickness cheesecloth-lined sieve set over bowl, drain 2 tubs (each 500 g) plain yogurt in refrigerator for at least 3 hours or up to 24 hours until reduced to about 2 cups (500 mL).

● Stir in 3 tbsp (50 mL) chopped green onions, 2 tbsp (25 mL) softened butter (if desired), 2 tsp (10 mL) crushed green peppercorns and 1/2 tsp (2 mL) each salt and crumbled dried thyme. Makes 2 cups (500 mL).

Ginger Shrimp on Oriental Noodles

An elegant little dinner for two revives romance any time of the year. Serve with tender crisp green beans brightened up with peppers and toasted sesame seeds.

12 oz	raw shrimp, peeled and deveined	375 g
1/3 cup	orange juice	75 mL
1/4 cup	lime juice	50 mL
2 tbsp	finely chopped onion	25 mL
2 tsp	minced gingerroot	10 mL
2 tsp	liquid honey	10 mL
1	clove garlic, minced	1
3/4 cup	chicken stock	175 mL
1 tsp	cornstarch	5 mL
4 tsp	butter	20 mL
8 oz	rice stick noodles	250 g
2 tsp	chopped fresh parsley	10 mL

● Place shrimp in small bowl. In measuring cup, whisk together orange juice, lime juice, onion, ginger, honey and garlic; pour half over shrimp, stirring to coat. Cover and let stand at room temperature for 30 minutes.

● Meanwhile, in small saucepan, heat remaining marinade with stock over medium-high heat; whisk in cornstarch and bring to boil. Reduce heat to medium; simmer for about 4 minutes or until thickened and glossy. Stir in 1 tbsp (15 mL) of the butter. Keep warm.

● In nonstick skillet, melt remaining butter over high heat; cook shrimp, turning once, for 3 to 4 minutes or just until pink.

● Meanwhile, in large pot of boiling salted water, cook noodles, stirring frequently, for about 3 minutes or until tender but firm. Drain and transfer to warmed platter; top with shrimp and drizzle with sauce. Sprinkle with parsley. Makes 2 servings.

Spicy Scallops ▶

Gingery and just a tad hot, these stir-fried scallops make a chic quick dinner with rice and steamed bok choy or broccoli.

2 tsp	vegetable oil	10 mL
3 tbsp	chopped green onions	50 mL
1 tbsp	minced gingerroot	15 mL
1 lb	scallops	500 g

	SAUCE	
	SAUCE	
2 tbsp	sherry	25 mL
1 tbsp	soy sauce	15 mL
1 tbsp	sesame oil	15 mL
1 tsp	granulated sugar	5 mL
1/2 tsp	chili paste or hot pepper sauce	2 mL

SOY SAUCE

Three kinds of soy sauce are available in supermarkets across the country.
● Light soy sauce is the one used in stir-fries, sauces and most of the recipes in this book. You'll know it's light soy sauce if you tip a bottle of it down, then back up, and notice that the soy sauce clears the glass almost immediately.
● The darker, thicker soy sauce that lingers as a translucent film over the glass is best suited to barbecue glazes.
● Sodium-reduced or "lite" soy sauce may be used in place of regular light soy sauce (above). Just add a little more to pump up the flavor.

● SAUCE: In small bowl, stir together sherry, soy sauce, sesame oil, sugar and chili paste; set aside.

● In nonstick skillet, heat vegetable oil over high heat; stir-fry onions and ginger for 10 seconds. Add scallops; stir-fry for 1 minute. Pour in sauce; stir-fry for 3 to 5 minutes or just until scallops are opaque. Makes 4 servings.

Dill-Grilled Salmon ▲

Slow-grilling salmon only on its skin side brings out all its natural succulence and saves on the flip-flop turning technique that can ruin delicate fish.

1 tbsp	minced onion	15 mL
1-1/2 tsp	lemon juice	7 mL
1	clove garlic, minced	1
2 tsp	chopped fresh dill	10 mL
1 tsp	olive oil	5 mL
Pinch	each salt and pepper	Pinch
4	salmon fillets (with skin), 1 inch (2.5 cm) thick	4

● Stir together onion, lemon juice, garlic, dill, oil, salt and pepper; rub half onto flesh side of salmon. Marinate at room temperature for 30 minutes.

● Place fish, skin side down, on lightly greased grill over low heat; cover and cook for 15 minutes.

● Uncover and brush with remaining marinade; increase heat to medium and cook for 10 minutes or until fish flakes easily when tested with fork. Makes 4 servings.

Pan-Fried Black Cod Fillets

2	dried Chinese or large button mushrooms, diced	2
1 lb	black cod fillets, about 3/4 inch (2 cm) thick	500 g
2 tbsp	cornstarch	25 mL
1 tbsp	vegetable oil	15 mL
2	green onions	2
3 tbsp	chicken stock	50 mL
1 tbsp	soy sauce	15 mL
1 tsp	granulated sugar	5 mL
1 tsp	sesame oil	5 mL
1/2 tsp	minced gingerroot	2 mL
1	clove garlic, minced	1

● Soak dried mushrooms in warm water for 20 minutes; drain well. Discard stems; finely chop caps. Pat fillets dry; dust all over with cornstarch.

● In large nonstick skillet, heat vegetable oil over medium-high heat; cook fillets for 2 minutes on each side or until browned. Transfer to warmed platter.

● Wipe out skillet; bring mushrooms, onions, stock, soy sauce, sugar, sesame oil, ginger and garlic to boil, stirring; boil for 30 seconds. Pour over fish. Makes 4 servings.

TIP: Black cod is also called sablefish. If black cod is unavailable, you can substitute sea bass fillets or steaks.

From Grand King Seafood Restaurant in Vancouver comes this quick, flavor-packed entrée. Serve over rice with steamed Chinese greens or spinach, green beans or sugar snap peas.

Easy Pad Thai

1	pkg (227 g) wide rice noodles	1
2 tbsp	vegetable oil	25 mL
6 oz	lean ground pork	175 g
1	sweet red pepper, chopped	1
3	cloves garlic, minced	3
1/4 tsp	hot pepper flakes	1 mL
6 oz	raw shrimp, peeled and deveined	175 g
1/3 cup	chicken stock	75 mL
3 tbsp	fish sauce	50 mL
2 tbsp	granulated sugar	25 mL
2 tbsp	each lime juice and ketchup	25 mL
1	egg, beaten	1
2 cups	bean sprouts	500 mL
2	green onions, chopped	2
1/4 cup	chopped fresh coriander	50 mL
2 tbsp	chopped peanuts	25 mL
2	limes, cut into wedges	2

● Soak noodles in warm water for 15 minutes; drain and set aside.

● In large wok or deep skillet, heat oil over high heat; stir-fry pork, red pepper, garlic and hot pepper flakes for 2 minutes. Add shrimp; stir-fry for 1 minute.

● Stir in stock, fish sauce, sugar, lime juice and ketchup; stir-fry for 1 minute. Add noodles; toss to combine.

● Drizzle in egg, tossing until egg is set. Add bean sprouts; toss. Sprinkle with onions, coriander and peanuts. Garnish with lime. Makes 4 servings.

It does take a little time to measure out the ingredients for this easy-to-like noodle dish from Thailand, but the cooking is a snap — and the whole meal is in the wok.

Chops on the Grill ▶

A subtle marinade delicately flavors lamb chops, pork chops, pork tenderloin or chicken breasts.

8	lamb chops, trimmed	8
1/4 cup	lime juice	50 mL
1 tbsp	minced gingerroot	15 mL
1 tbsp	olive oil	15 mL
2 tsp	fancy molasses or packed brown sugar	10 mL
1-1/4 tsp	dried thyme	6 mL
1	clove garlic, minced	1
1/2 tsp	pepper	2 mL

● Place chops in shallow glass dish. Combine lime juice, ginger, oil, molasses, thyme, garlic and pepper; pour over chops, turning to coat. Marinate in refrigerator for 1 hour, turning often.

● Reserving marinade, place chops on greased grill over medium-high heat; cook, basting occasionally with marinade, for 5 to 7 minutes on each side for medium-rare or until desired doneness. Makes 4 servings.

Roast Pork with Fennel and Garlic

Redolent with the heady Italian scents of fennel and garlic, this simple roast is ideal for entertaining and weeknight meals alike. Serve with green beans, roasted squash and mashed potatoes.

6	cloves garlic, chopped	6
3/4 tsp	salt	4 mL
1 tbsp	olive oil	15 mL
1 tsp	pepper	5 mL
1 tsp	fennel seeds	5 mL
2 lb	boneless pork loin roast	1 kg

● In small bowl and using fork, crush garlic with salt until in rough paste; mix in oil, pepper and fennel seeds.

● Cut slits over top and sides of roast; rub paste over roast. Place in shallow dish; cover and marinate in refrigerator for at least 8 hours or up to 24 hours. Let stand at room temperature for 30 minutes.

● Transfer roast to roasting pan. Roast in 325°F (160°C) oven for 90 minutes or until meat thermometer registers 160°F (70°C). Transfer to cutting board and tent with foil; let stand for 10 minutes before slicing thinly. Makes 4 to 6 servings.

Mexican Pork Loin Roast

Toasted sesame seeds and chili flavors spike up a roast pork. Serve with salsa, tortillas and rice jazzed up with sweet peppers and tomatoes.

2 tbsp	sesame seeds	25 mL
2 tbsp	chopped canned green chilies	25 mL
2 tbsp	cider vinegar	25 mL
3	cloves garlic, minced	3
1/4 tsp	each pepper and crushed hot pepper flakes	1 mL
1/4 tsp	cinnamon	1 mL
Pinch	cloves	Pinch
2 lb	boneless pork loin roast	1 kg

● In small skillet, toast sesame seeds over medium-high heat, shaking pan often, for 3 to 4 minutes or until golden.

● In small bowl, combine sesame seeds, chilies, vinegar, garlic, pepper, hot pepper flakes, cinnamon and cloves.

● Trim any fat from pork; place in roasting pan. Cut slits in top of pork; spread with sesame seed mixture.

● Pour hot water into pan to depth of 1/4 inch (5 mm). Roast in 325°F (160°C) oven for about 90 minutes or until meat thermometer registers 160°F (70°C). Transfer to cutting board and tent with foil; let stand for 10 minutes before slicing. Makes 4 to 6 servings.

Glazed Pork Tenderloin

A mustard glaze with a teasing curry taste makes this pork tenderloin a sure bet for backyard entertaining. Serve with noodles or rice and pineapple slices grilled alongside the tenderloin.

3 tbsp	hot prepared mustard	50 mL
2 tbsp	liquid honey	25 mL
1 tsp	curry powder	5 mL
1 tsp	lime juice	5 mL
1/2 tsp	salt	2 mL
1	clove garlic, sliced	1
2	pork tenderloins (12 oz/375 g each)	2

● Combine mustard, honey, curry powder, lime juice, salt and garlic.

● Tuck thin end of each tenderloin underneath and tie with string. Place in shallow glass dish; pour marinade over top. Let stand at room temperature for 30 minutes. Or, cover and marinate in refrigerator for up to 24 hours; let stand at room temperature for 30 minutes.

● Reserving marinade, place pork on greased grill over medium heat; cover and cook, turning and brushing occasionally with marinade, for 25 minutes or until meat thermometer registers 160°F (70°C). Transfer to cutting board and tent with foil; let stand for 5 minutes before slicing thinly. Makes 6 servings.

Cider-Baked Ribs ▼

There's a double whammy of cider and apples to sweeten this tender feast of ribs.

6 lb	pork spareribs	2.7 kg
2 cups	apple cider or juice	500 mL
1/2 cup	Dijon mustard	125 mL
1/4 cup	liquid honey	50 mL
1/4 cup	lemon juice	50 mL
2 tbsp	Worcestershire sauce	25 mL
1/2 tsp	pepper	2 mL
Dash	hot pepper sauce	Dash
4	Golden Delicious apples	4

● Cut spareribs into 3-rib pieces; trim off excess fat. Place in shallow roasting or broiler pan.

● Combine 1/4 cup (50 mL) of the cider, the mustard, honey, lemon juice, Worcestershire sauce, pepper and hot pepper sauce; brush half over ribs. Pour half of the remaining cider into pan.

● Bake in 375°F (190°C) oven for 1-1/2 hours, basting ribs occasionally with remaining mustard mixture, turning once and adding remaining cider as it evaporates.

● Core apples; cut each into 6 pieces. Arrange around ribs; baste with pan juices. Seal pan with foil; bake for 20 minutes or until apples are tender. *(Ribs can be prepared to this point, cooled in refrigerator and stored for up to 1 day; reheat in 350°F/180°C oven for 30 minutes.)*

● Transfer ribs and apples to warmed platter. Strain pan juices into bowl; skim off fat. Pour over ribs and apples. Makes 8 servings.

Sticky Pineapple Ribs ▲

3 lb	pork back spareribs	1.5 kg
1 cup	apricot jam	250 mL
1/4 cup	soy sauce	50 mL
2 tbsp	packed brown sugar	25 mL
2 tbsp	white wine vinegar	25 mL
2	cloves garlic, minced	2
1 tsp	ground ginger	5 mL
1/2 tsp	each salt and pepper	2 mL
1/4 tsp	cayenne pepper	1 mL
1	can (8 oz/227 g) pineapple tidbits	1

● Cut between bones to separate spareribs into ribs; trim off excess fat. Arrange in single layer in greased 13- x 9-inch (3 L) baking dish.

● Combine jam, soy sauce, sugar, vinegar, garlic, ginger, salt, pepper, cayenne and pineapple and juices; pour over ribs, turning to coat.

● Bake in 350°F (180°C) oven, basting every 15 minutes without turning, for 1-1/2 hours or until glazed and tender. Skim fat from sauce; serve with ribs. Makes 4 servings.

A *slow bake in a sweet-and-sour fruit glaze delivers all the flavor that ribs are famous for — without the lengthy marinating and precooking that most rib recipes require. One taste, and you'll know you've cooked up a guaranteed family pleaser.*

Peppered Leg of Lamb

For maximum tenderness, slice lamb across the grain and serve with barbecue-baked sweet potatoes and a romaine and cucumber salad.

3 lb	boneless leg of lamb	1.5 kg
2 tbsp	peppercorns, coarsely crushed	25 mL
4	cloves garlic	4
1/2 cup	dry white wine	125 mL
1/4 cup	olive oil	50 mL
1/2 tsp	salt	2 mL

● Pat lamb dry. Make several slashes in thickest part of meat; place in shallow glass dish.

● In blender or food processor, purée together peppercorns, garlic, wine and oil; pour over lamb. Cover and marinate in refrigerator for 2 hours or up to 8 hours, turning occasionally. Let stand at room temperature for 30 minutes.

● Reserving marinade, place lamb on greased grill over medium-high heat; cover and cook, turning and brushing with marinade every 10 minutes, for 40 minutes or until meat thermometer registers 140°F (60°C) for rare or until desired doneness.

● Transfer to cutting board; sprinkle with salt. Tent with foil and let stand for 10 minutes before slicing. Makes 8 servings.

TIP: To crush peppercorns, enclose in a piece of kitchen cloth and use a hammer or edge of heavy skillet or pan to crush.

Marinated Lamb Kabobs

Even though lamb shoulder takes a little more time to trim and cube, it's less expensive than leg and produces wonderfully juicy kabobs.

2 tbsp	red wine vinegar	25 mL
2 tsp	ground cumin	10 mL
1-1/2 tsp	each salt and ground coriander	7 mL
1 tsp	nutmeg	5 mL
1 tsp	grated lemon rind	5 mL
1/2 tsp	each cinnamon and dried oregano	2 mL
3	cloves garlic, minced	3
3 tbsp	olive oil	50 mL
2 lb	lean boneless lamb, cut into 2-inch (5 cm) cubes	1 kg
1	lemon, sliced	1
2	sweet red peppers, cut into chunks	2
1	onion, cut into wedges	1
12	button mushrooms	12

● In small bowl, combine vinegar, cumin, salt, coriander, nutmeg, lemon rind, cinnamon, oregano and garlic; gradually whisk in oil.

● In shallow glass dish, pour marinade over lamb and lemon, stirring to coat lamb. Cover and marinate in refrigerator for at least 8 hours or up to 24 hours, stirring occasionally. Let stand at room temperature for 30 minutes.

● Remove from marinade; discard lemon. Alternately thread lamb, red peppers, onion and mushrooms onto skewers. Place on greased grill over medium-high heat; cover and cook, turning once and brushing with remaining marinade, for 10 minutes or until lamb is still pink inside and vegetables are tender. Makes 6 servings.

Pacific Rim Flank Steak ▼

1 lb	flank steak	500 g
2 tbsp	hoisin sauce	25 mL
1 tbsp	each rice vinegar, sherry and liquid honey	15 mL
1 tsp	sesame oil	5 mL
1/2 tsp	grated orange rind	2 mL
3	cloves garlic, minced	3
Pinch	hot pepper flakes	Pinch

● Place steak in shallow dish or in plastic bag set in bowl. Combine hoisin sauce, vinegar, sherry, honey, oil, orange rind, garlic and hot pepper flakes; pour over steak. Cover and marinate in refrigerator for at least 12 hours or up to 24 hours, turning occasionally. Let stand at room temperature for 30 minutes.

● Discarding marinade, broil or grill steak for 5 to 7 minutes on each side or until medium-rare. Transfer to cutting board and tent with foil; let stand for 5 minutes. Slice thinly on angle across the grain. Makes 4 servings.

An Asian-inspired marinade piles on flavor as it tenderizes a lean cut of beef.

Grilled Sirloin with Roasted Garlic Aioli

Originally from the south of France, aioli is a garlicky mayonnaise that is now popular here as an accompaniment for fish, meat and vegetables. To round out this easy but very special warm-weather meal, bake potatoes on the barbecue while the garlic is roasting, pile a platter with sliced ripe red tomatoes and steam some corn and sugar snap peas.

3 lb	sirloin steak, 1-1/2 inches (4 cm) thick	1.5 kg
6	cloves garlic, quartered	6
	ROASTED GARLIC AIOLI	
1	whole garlic bulb	1
1 tbsp	olive oil	15 mL
3/4 cup	light mayonnaise	175 mL
Pinch	pepper	Pinch

● ROASTED GARLIC AIOLI: Cut top off garlic bulb, cutting through most cloves; peel off any papery skin. Place on small square of foil; drizzle with oil and fold up foil to seal. Place on greased grill over medium-high heat; cook for 30 minutes or until very soft. Unwrap and squeeze out garlic into bowl; mash with fork until smooth. Blend in mayonnaise and pepper.

● Meanwhile, cut 24 slits all over steak; insert garlic quarter into each. Place steak on grill; cook for 12 to 14 minutes on each side or until medium-rare. Transfer to cutting board and tent with foil; let stand for 5 minutes. Slice steak across the grain; serve with dollop of aioli. Makes 8 servings.

TIP: This sirloin makes enough for 8 party servings, but when your guest list is smaller, save the leftovers. Next day, simply slice the steak and pile it into split crusty buns slathered with the aioli — and, presto, supper's ready!

On-the-Barbecue Onion Pot Roast

Big and easy describes this lip-smacking new way with an economical cut of beef. Serve with a basket of fresh rolls and a bowl of greens for a relaxed weekend get-together.

5-1/2 lb	blade or chuck beef roast (bone in)	2.5 kg
2	onions	2
1/3 cup	red wine vinegar	75 mL
1/4 cup	Dijon mustard	50 mL
1/4 cup	olive oil	50 mL
1 tbsp	chopped fresh thyme (or 1 tsp/5 mL dried)	15 mL
2	bay leaves, crumbled	2
2	cloves garlic	2
1/4 tsp	each pepper and hot pepper sauce	1 mL

● Place roast in bowl. In food processor, purée together onions, vinegar, mustard, oil, thyme, bay leaves, garlic, pepper and hot pepper sauce; pour over roast. Cover and marinate in refrigerator for 24 hours, turning occasionally. Let stand at room temperature for 30 minutes.

● Reserving marinade, place roast on greased grill over high heat; cook, turning often, for 20 minutes or until browned.

● Turn off one burner; place roast over unlit burner. Increase heat to high on remaining burner; cover barbecue and cook roast, turning and basting occasionally with marinade, for 2-1/2 to 3 hours or until meat thermometer registers 160°F (70°C) for medium, or until desired doneness.

● Transfer to platter and tent with foil; let stand for 10 minutes before slicing. Makes 10 servings.

Pesto Chicken Pasta Salad

2 tbsp	pine nuts	25 mL
12	dry-packed sun-dried tomatoes	12
2	boneless skinless chicken breasts	2
1/3 cup	olive oil	75 mL
2 cups	tightly packed fresh basil leaves	500 mL
1/2 cup	freshly grated Parmesan cheese	125 mL
2	cloves garlic, minced	2
3/4 tsp	salt	4 mL
1/4 tsp	pepper	1 mL
5-1/2 cups	radiatore or rotini	1.375 L

● In large skillet, toast pine nuts over medium heat, shaking pan occasionally, for 6 minutes or until golden; remove and set aside.

● Meanwhile, cover tomatoes with boiling water; let stand for 3 to 5 minutes or until softened. Drain and cut into thin strips; set aside. Cut chicken crosswise into 1/4-inch (5 mm) thick strips.

● In skillet, heat 1 tbsp (15 mL) of the oil over medium-high heat; sauté chicken for 5 minutes or until no longer pink inside. Set aside.

● In food processor, purée basil with remaining oil; transfer to large bowl. Mix in Parmesan, garlic, salt, pepper, sun-dried tomatoes and chicken.

● Meanwhile, in large pot of boiling salted water, cook radiatore for 6 minutes or until tender but firm; drain, reserving 1/2 cup (125 mL) of the cooking water. Rinse under cold water; drain again.

● Toss pasta with basil mixture, adding a little of the cooking water to moisten, if desired. Garnish with pine nuts. Makes 6 servings.

This is the most requested salad at Hannah's Kitchen, a north Toronto café operated by the creative and energetic husband-and-wife team of Michael Shields and Susan Hughes. Serve with crusty bread and a toss of greens. (Photo, p. 32)

COOKING KNOW-HOW

When the recipe calls for one onion, does it mean small, medium or large? What's the difference between blanch and refresh? Here are the answers plus assumptions and cooking terms you will find helpful when following our recipes.

BASICS

● Unless otherwise specified in our recipes, fruits and vegetables, as well as the equipment called for, are medium-size.

● Eggs are large and should be at room temperature.

● Dried herbs are of the leaf, not ground, variety.

● Ovens are preheated.

● Saucepans are uncovered unless otherwise indicated.

TECHNIQUES

● **Blanch** means cooking fruits and vegetables briefly in boiling water to heighten color and flavor, loosen skins for peeling and to firm flesh.

● To **refresh**, plunge hot fruits or vegetables into cold water immediately to stop the cooking process and to retain color. Remove from water as soon as cooled.

● **Dredge** means to coat food lightly with flour or bread crumbs before frying to help brown the food.

● **Fold** is a gentle technique used to mix one ingredient into another, without beating or stirring, by gently lifting from underneath the mixture to overtop with a rubber spatula. Most commonly used in baking.

● **Sauté** by cooking food quickly in a small amount of fat in a skillet over direct heat, turning ingredients often.

● To **scald** a liquid, usually milk, warm over low or medium heat until small bubbles appear around the edge of the saucepan.

● **Simmer** means to cook food gently in liquid at a low enough temperature that only small bubbles appear on the surface.

● **Poach** is another gentle form of cooking food in liquid below the simmering point.

● **Julienne** foods by cutting them into thin, uniform-size matchstick strips.

Curry-Lime Barbecue Roast Chicken

Getting a whole chicken cooked through to the bone on the barbecue without charring the skin and drying out the breast is easy — just follow this recipe for pleasingly moist and golden-crisp results. Serve with a rice salad and a cool vegetable such as sliced cucumbers with a trim of mint.

1	chicken (4 lb/2 kg)	1
1	lime, halved	1
1 tsp	dried thyme	5 mL
1/4 cup	butter, softened	50 mL
1 tsp	grated lime rind	5 mL
1/4 cup	lime juice	50 mL
2 tsp	curry powder	10 mL

● Pat chicken dry; rub all over inside and out with lime. Sprinkle with thyme.

● Place chicken, breast side up, on greased grill over medium-high heat; cook, turning often, for 10 to 15 minutes or until browned.

● Turn off one burner; place chicken over unlit burner. Increase heat to high on remaining burner; cover barbecue and cook chicken for 1 hour, turning halfway through.

● Mash together butter, lime rind and juice and curry powder; brush over chicken. Cook chicken, turning and basting occasionally, for 30 to 60 minutes longer or until meat thermometer inserted in thickest part of thigh registers 185°F (85°C).

● Transfer to platter and tent with foil; let stand for 10 minutes before carving. Makes 6 servings.

Thai-Style Chicken

The mildly hot and spicy Asian flavors are beautifully balanced with a touch of sweet and citrus. Accompany with rice and a crisp green vegetable such as sugar snap peas, broccoli or beans.

1 tbsp	grated lime rind	15 mL
1/3 cup	lime juice	75 mL
1/4 cup	fish sauce	50 mL
3 tbsp	packed brown sugar	50 mL
2 tbsp	ketchup	25 mL
2 tbsp	hoisin sauce	25 mL
1 tbsp	minced gingerroot	15 mL
1 tbsp	chopped jalapeño pepper (or other hot pepper)	15 mL
2	cloves garlic, minced	2
4	each chicken breasts and legs, skinned	4

● In large bowl, combine lime rind and juice, fish sauce, sugar, ketchup, hoisin sauce, ginger, jalapeño pepper and garlic. Add chicken, turning to coat; cover and marinate in refrigerator for at least 4 hours or up to 8 hours, turning occasionally. Let stand at room temperature for 30 minutes.

● Discarding marinade, broil or grill chicken, turning once, for 8 to 10 minutes or until browned, breasts are no longer pink inside and juices run clear when legs are pierced. Makes 8 servings.

COOKING WITH HERBS

● In summer, fresh herbs are a delight. The easiest to grow and the most available at markets are parsley, dill, basil, thyme, sage, mint, rosemary, savory, oregano and marjoram.

● Fresh coriander (or cilantro, as it is often called) has become a fixture in urban Canadian markets but is still rare in smaller centers. Replace with fresh parsley or dried cilantro available in jars.

● When substituting dried herbs for fresh, use about one-third of the required amount. If using home-dried herbs, add a little more since the flavor is not as intense as bottled dried herbs.

● Always store herbs away from heat and light and replenish your supply frequently.

Chicken with Cumin and Garlic ▲

1 tbsp	vegetable oil	15 mL
2 lb	skinless chicken pieces	1 kg
1 tsp	ground cumin	5 mL
1/4 tsp	each salt, pepper and hot pepper flakes	1 mL
3	cloves garlic, minced	3
2	whole cloves	2
2 tsp	lemon or lime juice	10 mL
1/4 cup	chopped fresh coriander or parsley	50 mL

● In large nonstick skillet, heat oil over medium-high heat; brown chicken on all sides.

● Sprinkle cumin, salt, pepper and hot pepper flakes over chicken. Add 1 cup (250 mL) water, garlic, cloves and lemon juice. Reduce heat, cover and simmer for 15 minutes. Discard cloves. Remove chicken to platter; keep warm.

● Boil liquid in pan for about 5 minutes or until reduced to about 1/4 cup (50 mL). Stir in coriander. Spoon over chicken. Makes 4 servings.

Removing skin from chicken considerably reduces the amount of fat in a recipe without cutting back on any of the great taste. Play up the Mexican flavor of cumin with sweet corn and rice accented with chopped sweet red pepper and green onion.

Desserts on the Double

Here's plenty of inspiration for a touch of something sweet to end a meal, whether it's quick and weeknight, or weekend and company. And here's the bonus — these are all a cinch to make!

Baked Summer-Fruit Compote ▶

*T*his jewel-toned compote has just a touch of sugar to let the natural sweetness and flavor of the fruit medley shine. Serve over a wedge of angel cake or frozen yogurt, or spoon into stemmed glasses and top with Vanilla Custard Yogurt Sauce (recipe, p. 68).

3	peaches	3
3	apricots	3
3	plums	3
1/4 cup	granulated sugar	50 mL
12	strawberries or cherries	12
1/2 cup	blueberries	125 mL

● Remove pits from peaches, apricots and plums; cut fruit into large chunks and place in 8-inch (2 L) square baking dish. Sprinkle sugar over top. Bake in 350°F (180°C) oven for 20 minutes.

● Stir in strawberries and blueberries; cook for about 10 minutes or until fruit is tender. Stir gently. Let cool to room temperature. Makes 4 to 6 servings.

Honey Almond Nectarines

*A*maretti cookies are available in Italian and specialty food stores. Nut macaroons can be substituted.

4	nectarines	4
8	amaretti cookies	8
1/4 cup	liquid honey	50 mL
1/4 cup	water	50 mL
2 tsp	lemon juice	10 mL
1 cup	blackberries	250 mL

● Halve and pit nectarines; place, cut side up, in 9-inch (23 cm) pie plate. Crush cookies, leaving some larger pieces; mound in nectarine hollows.

● Combine honey, water and lemon juice. Pour half into pie plate; spoon remainder over crumbs. Bake in 375°F (190°C) oven, basting twice, for 15 to 20 minutes or until tender.

● Place 2 halves on each plate. Top each with a few berries; drizzle with juices. Serve warm. Makes 4 servings.

Melon with Lime and Mint

A variety of melons — cantaloupe, honeydew and red and yellow watermelons — create a dramatic presentation out of something simple and fresh. Garnish with extra sprigs of mint.

1/4 cup	granulated sugar	50 mL
1/4 cup	water	50 mL
1/4 cup	lime juice	50 mL
4 tsp	chopped fresh mint	20 mL
4 cups	cubed peeled melon	1 L

● In small saucepan, bring sugar and water to boil, stirring until sugar dissolves; boil for 2 minutes. Let cool.

● In bowl, stir together sugar syrup, lime juice and mint; add melon and stir gently. Refrigerate for at least 2 hours or until chilled. *(Fruit can be refrigerated for up to 8 hours.)* Makes 4 servings.

Broiled Peaches with Frozen Yogurt

Broil or even grill peaches for a luscious fork-and-spoon dessert.

2	large peaches	2
2 tbsp	orange juice	25 mL
	Brown sugar	
	Frozen yogurt	

● Halve and pit peaches; place, cut side up, in shallow baking dish. Spoon orange juice into hollows; sprinkle with sugar to taste.

● Broil for 3 to 5 minutes or until sugar is lightly caramelized. Transfer to serving dishes; top with scoop of frozen yogurt. Makes 4 servings.

TIP: To grill, combine orange juice and brown sugar and brush over cut sides of peaches, using any remaining juice to drizzle over peaches as they cook.

JUST PEACHY!

● When local tree-ripened peaches are available, there's no need to peel them before broiling or grilling. Just rub off fuzz with a rough tea towel.

● When peeling a large quantity of fully ripe peaches, immerse them for about 30 seconds in boiling water before peeling to loosen skins.

Rhubarb Fool

1-1/2 cups	Stewed Rhubarb (recipe, this page)	375 mL
1 cup	whipping cream	250 mL
8	strawberries	8

● In food processor, purée stewed rhubarb until smooth; transfer to serving bowl.

● Whip cream; gently fold into rhubarb, leaving streaks. *(Fool can be covered and refrigerated for up to 4 hours.)* Garnish each serving with strawberry. Makes 8 servings.

Ruby red or pink forced rhubarb is ideal for this company dessert, but garden rhubarb is just fine, too. Serve in pretty glass goblets.

Stewed Rhubarb

6 cups	chopped rhubarb	1.5 L
1 cup	granulated sugar	250 mL
2 tbsp	water	25 mL

● In large saucepan, combine rhubarb, sugar and water; cook over medium heat, stirring, until sugar has dissolved.

● Reduce heat to medium-low; simmer, stirring occasionally, for about 15 minutes or until slightly thickened and rhubarb is in threads. Let cool. *(Rhubarb can be refrigerated in airtight container for up to 5 days.)* Makes about 3 cups (750 mL).

In the spring and early summer, a bowl of stewed rhubarb is a classic Canadian dessert. Use it as a quick sauce for ice cream or as the base for other desserts such as Rhubarb Fool (recipe, this page).

Rhubarb and Berry Compote

1 cup	granulated sugar	250 mL
1/4 cup	water	50 mL
6 cups	chopped rhubarb	1.5 L
1	strip orange rind	1
1 cup	sliced strawberries	250 mL

● In top of double boiler over direct heat, bring sugar and water to boil. Place over boiling water in double boiler; stir in rhubarb and orange rind. Cover and cook over gently boiling water, without stirring, for 15 to 20 minutes or until tender.

● Turn off heat; let rhubarb cool in pan over hot water. Refrigerate until chilled. To serve, remove orange rind; gently stir in strawberries. Makes 4 servings.

A gentle cooking method lets the chunks of tender rhubarb keep their shape. Sliced strawberries add class to what's basically the country's most old-fashioned dessert.

Piña Colada Fool

Creamy yet refreshing, this pineapple treat is an ideal ending for any spicy Asian or Latin meal.

1 cup	drained unsweetened crushed pineapple	250 mL
1-1/2 cups	whipping cream	375 mL
1/2 cup	sweetened shredded coconut	125 mL
1 tbsp	coconut liqueur or rum (optional)	15 mL
	Mint sprigs (optional)	

● In blender or food processor, purée half of the pineapple; add to remaining pineapple. In separate bowl, whip cream; fold in pineapple, coconut, and coconut liqueur (if using).

● Divide among 6 long-stemmed glasses. Chill for 1 hour. Garnish with mint (if using). Makes 6 servings.

Mango Fool

This refreshing dessert has half the fat of a traditional fool made with fruit and cream. Serve garnished with sliced mango and mint leaves. If your cupboard holds a bottle of the alluring cardamom, a light dusting of this spice adds magic to mango.

1 cup	plain yogurt	250 mL
2	large mangoes, peeled and cubed	2
1 tbsp	lime juice	15 mL
1/3 cup	whipping cream	75 mL
1 tbsp	granulated sugar	15 mL

● In cheesecloth-lined sieve set over bowl, drain yogurt in refrigerator overnight to make about 1/2 cup (125 mL). Discard whey; transfer yogurt to bowl.

● In food processor, purée mangoes until smooth; whisk into yogurt along with lime juice.

● Whip cream with sugar; whisk one-quarter into mango mixture. Fold in remaining whipped cream. Refrigerate for at least 1 hour or up to 24 hours. Makes 6 servings.

Banana Brittle Sundaes

Familiar, yes, but this is still an amazingly simple and always pleasing dessert. A few chunks of peanut brittle add a flavorful crunch.

4 oz	peanut brittle	125 g
4	firm bananas	4
2/3 cup	packed brown sugar	150 mL
1/4 cup	butter	50 mL
2 tbsp	each lemon juice and dark rum	25 mL
4 cups	vanilla ice cream	1 L

● In blender or food processor, coarsely chop peanut brittle. Cut bananas in half crosswise, then lengthwise.

● In large skillet, combine sugar, butter, lemon juice, rum and 2 tbsp (25 mL) water; bring to boil over medium heat. Add bananas, gently turning to coat.

● Reduce heat and simmer, spooning sauce over bananas, for 2 to 3 minutes or until heated through but still firm.

● Spoon ice cream into chilled bowls; top with banana mixture. Sprinkle with peanut brittle. Makes 8 servings.

Blueberry Frozen Yogurt

2 cups	blueberries	500 mL
1/3 cup	granulated sugar	75 mL
1 tsp	lemon juice	5 mL
2 cups	plain yogurt	500 mL

● In saucepan, combine blueberries, sugar, lemon juice and 2 tbsp (25 mL) water; cook over medium heat, stirring, until sugar dissolves. Reduce heat and simmer, stirring frequently, for about 3 minutes or until blueberries are softened.

● In food processor, purée blueberry mixture for 15 to 20 seconds or until smooth. Pour into bowl; refrigerate for 20 to 30 minutes or until cooled. Stir in yogurt.

● Pour into 13- x 9-inch (3 L) metal baking dish; cover and freeze for 3 or 4 hours or until almost firm. Break up and blend, in batches, in food processor until smooth. Transfer to chilled airtight container; freeze for at least 1 hour or until firm. *(Yogurt can be stored in freezer for up to 2 days.)* Makes 4 servings.

No, you don't need an ice-cream machine to make your own fresh frozen yogurts. This short recipe shows how easy it is to use a baking pan and food processor for an unbelievably creamy frozen dessert. Serve with extra blueberries.

Individual Summer Puddings

7 cups	fresh berries (raspberries, blackberries and blueberries)	1.75 L
1/3 cup	granulated sugar	75 mL
1 tbsp	lemon juice	15 mL
12	soft ladyfingers	12

● Reserve 1 cup (250 mL) berries for garnish. In nonaluminum saucepan, combine remaining berries, sugar and lemon juice; cover and cook over medium-low heat, stirring occasionally, for 7 to 10 minutes or until softened and juicy but not mushy.

● Cut each ladyfinger into thirds; place 2 pieces in each of six 3/4-cup (175 mL) stemmed glasses. Spoon scant 1/4 cup (50 mL) fruit mixture over top. Repeat layers twice, pressing with back of spoon.

● Cover and refrigerate for at least 2 hours or up to 1 day. Let stand at room temperature for 1 hour before serving. Garnish with reserved berries. Makes 6 servings.

Here's a fresh take on the classic English fruit-and-bread pudding that chills and sets overnight. Ladyfingers replace the more mundane bread. In a pinch, you can substitute 3 cups (750 mL) cubed sponge or pound cake.

Strawberry Crème Brûlée

8 cups	strawberries, hulled	2 L
2 tbsp	rum	25 mL
2 cups	whipping cream	500 mL
3/4 cup	packed brown sugar	175 mL

● Halve strawberries; place in shallow 12-cup (3 L) baking dish. Drizzle with rum. Whip cream; spread over berries.

● Press sugar through sieve to cover whipped cream evenly; cover with plastic wrap. Refrigerate for at least 8 hours or up to 12 hours.

● To serve, broil for about 2 minutes or until sugar is crisp and caramel-colored. Serve immediately. Makes 12 servings.

This decadent and too-easy-to-be-believed way to serve berries and cream is adapted from a peach dessert presented over the years by food writer and author Rose Murray to her many fortunate guests.

Chocolate Raspberry Mousse

With frozen raspberries, you can whip up this impressive little dessert any time of year. For a dazzling presentation, add a generous sprinkle of fresh or barely thawed unsweetened berries and lightly whipped cream mixed with yogurt.

6 oz	semisweet or bittersweet chocolate, chopped	175 g
1/3 cup	packed fresh or thawed raspberries	75 mL
3/4 cup	whipping cream	175 mL
	Icing sugar	

● In top of double boiler over hot (not boiling) water, melt chocolate; transfer to large bowl and let cool completely, stirring occasionally.

● In food processor, purée raspberries; press through fine mesh sieve to make about 1/4 cup (50 mL) purée. Stir into cooled chocolate.

● In bowl, whip cream; whisk one-quarter into chocolate mixture. Fold in remaining whipped cream.

● Lightly grease and line bottoms of four 1/2-cup (125 mL) ramekins or custard cups, or one 2-cup (500 mL) pâté mould, with parchment paper rounds. Spoon in mousse. Cover and refrigerate for about 2 hours or until firm. *(Mousse can be refrigerated for up to 2 days.)*

● Turn out onto dessert plates; remove paper and dust with icing sugar. Makes 4 servings.

Chocolate Fudge Pudding

Who can resist this self-saucing pudding, its cake-like topping rising out of a fudgy chocolate sauce?

1 cup	all-purpose flour	250 mL
2/3 cup	granulated sugar	150 mL
3 tbsp	unsweetened cocoa powder	50 mL
2 tsp	baking powder	10 mL
1 tsp	salt	5 mL
2 tsp	butter	10 mL
1/2 cup	chopped nuts	125 mL
1 cup	milk	250 mL
1-1/2 tsp	vanilla	7 mL
	SAUCE	
3/4 cup	packed brown sugar	175 mL
2 tbsp	unsweetened cocoa powder	25 mL
1-3/4 cups	boiling water	425 mL

● In bowl, mix together flour, sugar, cocoa, baking powder and salt; with pastry blender or two knives, cut in butter until in coarse crumbs. Stir in nuts. Add milk and vanilla, stirring to mix well. Spoon into greased 6-cup (1.5 L) saucepan or 8-inch (2 L) square cake pan.

● SAUCE: Combine brown sugar and cocoa; sprinkle over batter. Pour boiling water over top.

● Cover and cook over medium heat or bake, uncovered, in 350°F (180°C) oven for 30 to 35 minutes or until top is firm to the touch. Let stand for 10 minutes. Makes 6 servings.

CHOCOLATE FONDUE

● Chop 6 oz (175 g) bittersweet or semisweet chocolate and 4 oz (125 g) milk chocolate; place in fondue pot. Heat 3/4 cup (175 mL) whipping cream to boiling; pour over chocolate, whisking until smooth. Add 2 tbsp (25 mL) brandy or rum, or 1 tsp (5 mL) vanilla. Set over warmer and provide strawberries, banana, papaya or pineapple chunks, dried apricot halves, ripe pears or cubes of pound cake for dipping.

Fresh Berry Pudding

1	small banana	1
1 cup	sliced strawberries	250 mL
1/2 cup	raspberries	125 mL
1 tbsp	packed brown sugar	15 mL
1/2 cup	plain yogurt	125 mL
1/2 cup	blueberries	125 mL

● In food processor or blender, purée together banana, strawberries, raspberries and sugar until smooth; transfer to bowl. Fold in yogurt.

● Spoon into serving dishes; sprinkle with blueberries. Cover and refrigerate for at least 1 hour or until chilled. Makes 4 servings.

Nutritious, delicious — and uncomplicated! This slightly tart purée of fruit and yogurt will make you realize just how good creamy custard puddings can taste.

Apple Berry Clafouti

4 cups	thinly sliced apples	1 L
1/2 cup	frozen raspberries or cranberries	125 mL
1/3 cup	granulated sugar	75 mL
3	eggs	3
1 cup	milk	250 mL
1/2 cup	all-purpose flour	125 mL
2 tsp	vanilla	10 mL
1/4 tsp	each nutmeg and salt	1 mL
2 tbsp	packed brown sugar	25 mL

● In bowl, toss apples and raspberries with half of the granulated sugar; spread evenly in greased 10-inch (25 cm) pie plate.

● In separate bowl, whisk together remaining granulated sugar, eggs, milk, flour, vanilla, nutmeg and salt until smooth; pour over fruit.

● Bake in 350°F (180°C) oven for about 40 minutes or until puffed and set. Sprinkle with brown sugar; broil for about 3 minutes or until dark golden. Serve warm. Makes 6 servings.

This tangy-sweet custard dessert is easier to make than an apple pie (and lighter, too!).

Winter Fruit Crisp ◄

6	large apples (preferably Golden Delicious)	6
3	pears (preferably Bosc)	3
1/2 cup	halved dried apricots	125 mL
1/2 cup	halved prunes or dates	125 mL
1/2 cup	raisins or currants	125 mL
3 tbsp	lemon juice	50 mL
2 tbsp	packed brown sugar	25 mL
2 tbsp	butter, cut into bits	25 mL
	TOPPING	
3/4 cup	all-purpose flour	175 mL
1/2 cup	packed brown sugar	125 mL
1 tbsp	cinnamon	15 mL
1/2 cup	butter	125 mL
1/2 cup	each rolled oats and chopped walnuts	125 mL

● Peel, core and slice apples and pears. In large bowl, toss together apples, pears, apricots, prunes and raisins. Sprinkle with lemon juice, sugar and butter; toss again. Transfer to greased 13- x 9-inch (3 L) baking dish, leveling top.

● TOPPING: In bowl, combine flour, sugar and cinnamon; with pastry blender or two knives, cut in butter until crumbly. Stir in oats and walnuts; sprinkle over fruit.

● Bake in 375°F (190°C) oven for 1 hour or until apples are tender. Makes 12 servings.

Dried fruits bolster winter's store of apples and pears for a dessert that begs second helpings. If dried cherries or cranberries are available, they make a colorful and tangy addition.

Autumn Cobbler

4 cups	chopped peeled pears	1 L
4 cups	chopped plums	1 L
2	large sprigs fresh rosemary	2
1/2 cup	granulated sugar	125 mL
1/2 cup	apple juice	125 mL
1 tbsp	cornstarch	15 mL
	TOPPING	
1/2 cup	butter	125 mL
3/4 cup	packed brown sugar	175 mL
1	egg	1
1-1/2 cups	all-purpose flour	375 mL
1/2 tsp	baking soda	2 mL
Pinch	salt	Pinch
3/4 cup	buttermilk	175 mL
1/2 cup	chopped pecans	125 mL

● In heavy saucepan, bring pears, plums, rosemary, sugar, apple juice and cornstarch to boil; reduce heat and simmer, stirring occasionally, for about 5 minutes or until thickened. Pour into greased 13- x 9-inch (3 L) baking dish.

● TOPPING: In bowl, beat butter with brown sugar until fluffy; beat in egg. Combine flour, baking soda and salt; stir into batter alternately with buttermilk, making three additions of flour mixture and two of buttermilk.

● Spoon batter into 8 portions around edge of fruit, leaving center uncovered. Sprinkle with pecans; bake in 375°F (190°C) oven for about 35 minutes or until browned and bubbly. Makes 8 servings.

From the Calgary bistro, Foodsmith, comes this delicious cobbler starring pears, plums and a surprise ingredient — fresh rosemary. You may be skeptical, but it's a must addition.

Slice-and-Bake Almond Crisps

First they were icebox, then refrigerator cookies. Now the freezer takes over this kind of handy treat. The dough is shaped into logs and chilled for slicing and baking at the convenience of the cook.

1 cup	butter, softened	250 mL
1/2 cup	packed brown sugar	125 mL
1/2 cup	granulated sugar	125 mL
1	egg	1
1 tsp	vanilla	5 mL
2-1/3 cups	all-purpose flour	575 mL
1/2 tsp	baking soda	2 mL
1/2 tsp	salt	2 mL
1-1/4 cups	toasted chopped unblanched almonds	300 mL

● In large bowl, beat together butter, brown sugar and granulated sugar until light and fluffy; beat in egg and vanilla.

● Combine flour, baking soda and salt; gradually beat into butter mixture. Stir in almonds. Shape into four 5-inch (10 cm) long logs. Wrap and freeze for 2 hours or until firm. *(Logs can be frozen for up to 6 weeks; slice and bake frozen.)*

● Cut into slices about 1/8 inch (3 mm) thick; bake on greased baking sheet in 375°F (190°C) oven for 8 to 10 minutes or until golden. Remove to rack and let cool. *(Cookies can be stored in airtight container for up to 1 week or frozen for up to 1 month.)* Makes 20 cookies per log.

Vanilla Custard Yogurt Sauce

This is a lighter version of crème anglaise, old-fashioned "pouring custard" in English. It's divine over fresh fruit, baked apples, crisps and pies.

1/2 cup	milk	125 mL
1-1/2 tsp	cornstarch	7 mL
1	egg yolk	1
2 tbsp	granulated sugar	25 mL
1-1/2 tsp	vanilla	7 mL
1/2 cup	plain yogurt	125 mL

● In saucepan, whisk together milk and cornstarch; whisk in egg yolk and sugar until well blended. Cook over medium heat, stirring constantly, for 3 to 5 minutes or until bubbly and thickened. Remove from heat; stir in vanilla.

● Transfer to bowl; place plastic wrap directly on surface. Refrigerate for about 45 minutes or until cool. Stir in yogurt. *(Sauce can be refrigerated in airtight container for up to 3 days.)* Makes 1 cup (250 mL).

Crème Anglaise

Here's the traditional version of the versatile vanilla custard. Try serving it over fruit crisps or pies instead of ice cream. It's very British — and very delish!

4	egg yolks	4
1/3 cup	granulated sugar	75 mL
1-3/4 cups	light cream	425 mL
2 tsp	vanilla	10 mL

● In bowl, beat egg yolks with sugar until thick and lemon-colored and mixture falls in ribbons when beaters are lifted.

● In heavy saucepan, heat cream almost to boiling. Whisk about half of hot cream into egg mixture, then pour back into saucepan.

● Cook over medium-low heat, stirring constantly with wooden spoon, for about 15 minutes or until thick enough to coat back of spoon. Do not boil.

● Strain through fine sieve into bowl. Stir in vanilla. Cover surface of sauce directly with plastic wrap to prevent skin from forming. Makes 2 cups (500 mL).

Lemon Mint Sauce

1/4 cup	granulated sugar	50 mL
1/4 cup	lightly packed fresh mint leaves	50 mL
1/4 cup	boiling water	50 mL
1/4 cup	lemon juice	50 mL

● In blender, mix together sugar, mint, water and lemon juice for 30 seconds or until mint is finely chopped. Refrigerate for at least 15 minutes or until cooled. *(Sauce can be refrigerated in airtight container for up to 2 days.)* Makes 2/3 cup (150 mL).

This is it, a delectable dressing for peaches, nectarines and melons — with nary a calorie from fat.

Cranberry Coffee Cake

1	pkg (250 g) cream cheese, softened	1
1-1/2 cups	granulated sugar	375 mL
1 cup	butter, softened	250 mL
1-1/2 tsp	vanilla	7 mL
4	eggs	4
2-1/4 cups	all-purpose flour	550 mL
1-1/2 tsp	baking powder	7 mL
1/2 tsp	salt	2 mL
1/4 tsp	nutmeg	1 mL
2-1/2 cups	cranberries	625 mL
1/2 cup	chopped pecans	125 mL
1 tbsp	icing sugar	15 mL

● In large bowl, beat together cream cheese, sugar, butter and vanilla until smooth; beat in eggs, one at a time. Combine 2 cups (500 mL) of the flour, baking powder, salt and nutmeg; add to batter in three additions.

● Toss together cranberries, pecans and remaining flour; fold into batter. Spoon into greased 10-inch (3 L) Bundt pan.

● Bake in 350°F (180°C) oven for 55 to 65 minutes or until tester inserted in center comes out clean. Let cool in pan for 15 minutes; turn out onto rack. Dust with icing sugar. Makes 12 to 16 servings.

Here's a gem of a dessert from the Richmond Nature Park Society in Richmond, B.C., where 80 per cent of Canada's cranberries are harvested.

Strawberry Icebox Cake

2 cups	strawberries	500 mL
1 cup	whipping cream	250 mL
2 tbsp	granulated sugar	25 mL
1/2 cup	plain yogurt	125 mL
42	chocolate wafers	42

● Mash half of the strawberries; drain, reserving juice for another use. In bowl, whip cream with sugar; fold in yogurt. Remove half to another bowl; fold in mashed strawberries.

● Spread one side of each of 6 wafers with about 2 tsp (10 mL) strawberry mixture. Stack wafers on top of one another; top stack with plain wafer. Repeat with remaining wafers to make 6 stacks.

● On platter, lay each stack on its side, with sides touching, to form rectangle. Spread with remaining whipped cream mixture to cover completely.

● Stand toothpicks on top to support paper; wrap and refrigerate for at least 4 hours or up to 8 hours. Halve remaining strawberries and arrange over top. Slice diagonally to serve. Makes 8 servings.

Entertaining is made easier with desserts like this no-bake log cake you can put together early in the day and serve with a flourish.

Banana Split Ice Cream Cake ◄

4 cups	strawberry ice cream	1 L
1/3 cup	chocolate sauce, chilled	75 mL
4 cups	vanilla ice cream	1 L
1	can (14 oz/398 mL) pineapple chunks	1
4 cups	chocolate ice cream	1 L
1/2 cup	whipping cream	125 mL
1 tbsp	icing sugar	15 mL
1	banana, sliced	1
	Maraschino cherries and fresh strawberries (optional)	
	STRAWBERRY SAUCE	
1-1/4 cups	frozen strawberries	300 mL
3 tbsp	granulated sugar	50 mL
1/2 tsp	grated orange rind	2 mL
1 tbsp	orange juice or water	15 mL
1 tsp	cornstarch	5 mL

● Let strawberry ice cream stand at room temperature for about 20 minutes or until spreadable; pack evenly into 9-inch (23 cm) springform pan. Pour chocolate sauce over top. Freeze for 15 to 20 minutes or until firm.

● Meanwhile, let vanilla ice cream stand at room temperature for about 20 minutes or until softened. Drain pineapple and purée in food processor; mix into vanilla ice cream. Spread over chocolate layer; freeze for 30 minutes or until firm.

● Meanwhile, let chocolate ice cream stand at room temperature for about 20 minutes or until softened; spread over pineapple layer. Freeze for 20 minutes or until set. *(Cake can be prepared to this point, covered and stored in freezer for up to 3 days.)*

● STRAWBERRY SAUCE: In small saucepan, stir together strawberries, sugar and orange rind. Blend orange juice with cornstarch; stir into pan and cook, stirring, over medium-high heat for 7 to 8 minutes or until thickened. Refrigerate until chilled.

● Whip cream with icing sugar; pipe or spoon decoratively over top of cake. Remove side of pan; garnish with banana slices, and maraschino cherries and strawberries (if using). Serve with strawberry sauce. Makes 12 servings.

With dessert in the freezer, it's easy to invite friends over. This fun fruit-trimmed cake, inspired by the ever-popular sundae, makes a great party or birthday cake.

Mocha Ricotta Cake

2 tbsp	instant coffee granules	25 mL
4 tsp	vanilla	20 mL
2 cups	ricotta cheese	500 mL
1/3 cup	granulated sugar	75 mL
1/4 cup	unsweetened cocoa powder, sifted	50 mL
Pinch	cinnamon	Pinch
1	angel food cake (7-1/2 inches/19 cm)	1

● In bowl, dissolve coffee in vanilla; whisk in ricotta, sugar, cocoa and cinnamon until smooth.

● Using serrated knife, cut cake crosswise into 5 layers. Place bottom layer on cake plate.

● Reserve half of the ricotta mixture; spread one-quarter of the remaining mixture over bottom layer. Repeat layering with remaining cake and filling.

● Spread reserved ricotta mixture over top and sides of cake. Cover and refrigerate for at least 2 hours or up to 12 hours. Makes 10 servings.

Ricotta cheese makes a creamy but light Italian-style filling in this make-ahead cake.

Honey Cardamom Coffee Cake ▶

Y*ou don't have to wait for Valentine's Day to bake a remarkably delicious cake for the people you love most.*

TIP: To bake in a heart shape, use a pan with a 10-cup (2.5 L) capacity.

1 cup	liquid honey	250 mL
1/2 cup	butter, softened	125 mL
2	eggs	2
1 tsp	vanilla	5 mL
2 cups	all-purpose flour	500 mL
1 tsp	baking powder	5 mL
1 tsp	ground cardamom	5 mL
1/2 tsp	each baking soda and salt	2 mL
2/3 cup	sour cream	150 mL
	STREUSEL TOPPING	
1/2 cup	sliced almonds	125 mL
1/3 cup	packed brown sugar	75 mL
1/3 cup	all-purpose flour	75 mL
2 tbsp	butter	25 mL
	ICING	
1/2 tsp	cinnamon	2 mL
2/3 cup	icing sugar	150 mL
2 tsp	milk	10 mL

● In bowl, beat honey with butter until smooth; beat in eggs, one at a time. Beat in vanilla. Stir together flour, baking powder, cardamom, baking soda and salt; add to honey mixture alternately with sour cream, making three additions of dry mixture and two of sour cream. Spoon into greased 9-inch (2.5 L) springform pan, smoothing top.

● STREUSEL TOPPING: In small bowl, stir together almonds, sugar and flour; with pastry blender or two knives, cut in butter until crumbly. Sprinkle over batter.

● Bake in 350°F (180°C) oven for about 1 hour or until cake tester inserted in center comes out clean. Let cool in pan on rack for 15 minutes. Remove from pan; let cool completely.

● ICING: Sprinkle cinnamon over cake. Whisk icing sugar with milk until smooth; drizzle over cake. Makes 10 servings.

Marble Chocolate Brownies

O*ur Test Kitchen has been experimenting with the new granular low-calorie sweetener with sucralose (Splenda) to create lower-calorie treats such as these dense brownies.*

1/4 cup	butter, softened	50 mL
2	eggs	2
1 tsp	vanilla	5 mL
1/2 cup	unsweetened applesauce	125 mL
2/3 cup	all-purpose flour	150 mL
1/2 cup	granular low-calorie sweetener with sucralose (Splenda)	125 mL
1 tsp	baking powder	5 mL
1/4 tsp	salt	1 mL
1/4 cup	unsweetened cocoa powder	50 mL

● In large bowl, beat together butter, eggs and vanilla for 1 minute; beat in applesauce just until blended. Combine flour, sweetener, baking powder and salt; fold into butter mixture just until moistened.

● Using 1/3 cup (75 mL) of the batter, drop by spoonfuls into greased 8-inch (2 L) square cake pan. Fold cocoa powder into remaining batter just until combined; gently spoon into pan, covering white batter and smoothing surface.

● Bake in 350°F (180°C) oven for 15 minutes or until cake tester inserted in center comes out clean. Let cool in pan on rack. Cut into squares. Makes 16 squares.

Breakfast & Lunch

From one-minute Pancake Sandwiches to pack-and-go Minestrone Salad and Thermos-friendly Bacon and Egg Chowder, here's our pick of nutritious quick fixes to see you through the day.

Best-Ever Pancakes ▶

Fresh or make-ahead and frozen, pancakes are a delicious start to any day. Serve with favorite toppings — or try our nifty Pancake Sandwiches (below).

2 cups	Best Pancake Mix (recipe, p. 77)	500 mL
1 cup	water	250 mL
1	egg, lightly beaten	1
1/4 tsp	nutmeg	1 mL
	Melted butter	

● In bowl and using fork, stir together Best Pancake Mix, water, egg and nutmeg until blended.

● Heat griddle over medium-high heat; brush with butter. Using 1/4 cup (50 mL) batter for each pancake and brushing griddle with more butter as necessary, pour batter onto griddle; cook for about 2 minutes or until golden brown on bottom and bubbles break on top but do not fill in.

● Using spatula, turn and cook for about 1 minute or until bottom is golden brown. (*Pancakes can be layered between waxed paper, wrapped well in plastic wrap and frozen in airtight container or freezer bag for up to 2 weeks.*) Makes nine 4-inch (20 cm) pancakes.

ONE-MINUTE PANCAKE SANDWICHES

With pancakes in the freezer, it's easy to whip up a quick and nutritious portable breakfast the whole family will enjoy. Simply pop frozen pancakes into a toaster or toaster oven and warm through, then sandwich together with your choice of flavorful fillings. Serve with a glass of milk and you have a complete meal.

● **Piggie in a Blanket:** In nonstick skillet, cook 1 breakfast sausage over medium-high heat, or microwave at High for 2 minutes, or until no longer pink inside. Spread 1 pancake with 1-1/2 tsp (7 mL) maple syrup; wrap pancake around sausage, securing with toothpick.

● **Fruit and Cheese:** Thinly slice one-quarter of an apple or pear and 1 oz (25 g) Cheddar cheese; sandwich between 2 pancakes.

● **Honey and Banana:** Spread 1 tbsp (15 mL) creamed honey evenly over 2 pancakes; top 1 with half a thinly sliced banana. Sandwich together.

● **Cream Cheese and Raisin:** Spread 2 tbsp (25 mL) spreadable cream cheese evenly over 2 pancakes; sprinkle with 1 tbsp (15 mL) raisins. Sandwich together.

Upside-Down Apple Pancake ▲

A *delicate puffed pancake baked with a layer of cinnamon-scented apples makes an impressive brunch dish for guests. The surprise for the cook is that something so pretty is also so easy — and so delicious!*

2 tbsp	butter	25 mL
1/4 cup	granulated sugar	50 mL
2 tsp	cinnamon	10 mL
3	apples, peeled and sliced	3
	BATTER	
1/3 cup	all-purpose flour	75 mL
1/2 tsp	baking powder	2 mL
2	egg yolks	2
1/3 cup	milk	75 mL
4	egg whites	4
1/3 cup	granulated sugar	75 mL

● In two 9-inch (23 cm) pie plates or in a 13- x 9-inch (3 L) baking dish, heat butter in 400°F (200°C) oven for 2 minutes or until melted. Combine sugar and cinnamon; sprinkle over butter and bake for 2 minutes. Arrange sliced apples over top; bake for 10 minutes.

● BATTER: In bowl, combine flour and baking powder; blend in egg yolks and milk. In large bowl, beat egg whites until soft peaks form; gradually beat in sugar until stiff peaks form. Fold into milk mixture; spread evenly over apples.

● Bake for 15 to 20 minutes or until lightly browned. Loosen edges with knife; invert onto serving plate. Makes 6 servings.

Peanut Butter Roll-Ups

2	small flour tortillas	2
1/4 cup	peanut butter	50 mL
1	banana, sliced	1

● Spread each tortilla with half of the peanut butter; top with banana slices. Roll up into tubes. Makes 2 servings.

Trendy tortillas offer total portability to a favorite breakfast combo.

Cinnamon Tortillas with Strawberry Salsa

4	flour tortillas	4
2 tbsp	butter, melted	25 mL
2 tbsp	granulated sugar	25 mL
3/4 tsp	cinnamon	4 mL
	STRAWBERRY SALSA	
2 cups	strawberries, chopped	500 mL
1 tbsp	chopped fresh mint	15 mL
1/2 tsp	grated lime rind	2 mL
1 tbsp	lime juice	15 mL
1-1/2 tsp	liquid honey	7 mL

● STRAWBERRY SALSA: Combine strawberries, mint, lime rind and juice and honey; cover and refrigerate for 1 hour.

● Brush both sides of each tortilla with butter. Combine sugar and cinnamon; sprinkle over each side of tortilla.

● Bake on lightly greased baking sheet in 375°F (190°C) oven for about 10 minutes or until crisp and golden. Cut into quarters. Serve with salsa. Makes 4 servings.

Sweet, tart and minty, this chunky salsa is a great foil for cinnamon-crisped tortillas — perfect for brunch or afternoon tea.

Canadian Living's Best Pancake Mix

This mix makes the lightest and tenderest pancakes because it's made with soft low-gluten cake-and-pastry flour. It's also less expensive than bought pancake mixes and just as handy. Best of all, it takes just minutes to put together.

9 cups	sifted cake-and-pastry flour	2.25 L
1 cup	skim milk powder	250 mL
1/2 cup	granulated sugar	125 mL
1/4 cup	baking powder	50 mL
1 tbsp	salt	15 mL
2 tsp	baking soda	10 mL
1 lb	shortening	500 g

● In large bowl, stir together flour, milk powder, sugar, baking powder, salt and baking soda. Using pastry blender, cut in shortening until in fine crumbs.

● Transfer to airtight container; store in refrigerator for up to 2 months. Stir well before using. Makes about 15 cups (3.75 L).

Whole Wheat Waffles

Kids think it's magic the way waffles turn out with all those wonderful little pockets that catch the syrup. Get them involved in beating the egg whites — it's a bit of wizardry, too!

1 cup	all-purpose flour	250 mL
1/2 cup	whole wheat flour	125 mL
2 tbsp	granulated sugar	25 mL
2 tsp	baking powder	10 mL
1/4 tsp	baking soda	1 mL
1/4 tsp	cinnamon	1 mL
3	eggs, separated	3
1-3/4 cups	buttermilk or plain yogurt	425 mL
1/2 cup	butter, melted	125 mL
1/2 tsp	vanilla	2 mL
	Banana Nut Sauce (recipe, this page) or maple syrup	

● In large bowl, stir together all-purpose and whole wheat flours, sugar, baking powder, baking soda and cinnamon; make large well in center. Pour egg yolks, buttermilk, butter and vanilla into well; using whisk, stir into flour mixture.

● In separate bowl, beat egg whites until soft peaks form; fold one-quarter into batter. Fold in remaining whites.

● Heat waffle machine and cook according to manufacturer's directions. For regular waffle maker, use 1/3 cup (75 mL) batter for each waffle; for deep Belgian waffle maker, use 1 cup (250 mL) batter. Serve with Banana Nut Sauce. Makes 12 regular waffles or 6 Belgian waffles, enough for 6 servings.

Banana Nut Sauce

Pretty nice over waffles and pancakes, this rich fruity sauce is also tasty over ice cream or frozen yogurt.

2 tbsp	butter	25 mL
1/2 cup	packed brown sugar	125 mL
1/2 cup	pineapple juice or orange juice	125 mL
4	bananas	4
1/2 tsp	cinnamon	2 mL
1/4 cup	chopped pecans or raisins	50 mL

● In skillet, melt butter over medium heat; stir in sugar and pineapple juice. Bring to boil; cook, stirring, for 1 to 2 minutes or until clear and slightly thickened.

● Meanwhile, slice bananas; add to skillet along with cinnamon. Cook for 1 minute or until bananas are heated through. Stir in pecans. Serve warm. Makes 2-1/2 cups (625 mL).

MEASURING DRY INGREDIENTS

When measuring flour, sugar and other dry ingredients, always use dry measures.

● The **imperial** set is made up of measuring spoons — 1/4 teaspoon (tsp), 1/2 tsp, 1 tsp and 1 tablespoon (tbsp). Three tsp make 1 tbsp. There are also dry measuring cups in 1/4-cup, 1/3-cup, 1/2-cup and 1-cup sizes.

● Measuring cups for dry ingredients are usually plastic or metal and need to be filled level to the top to make up the amount.

● **Metric** small measures (spoons) give 1, 2, 5 and 15 mL to compare roughly

with the imperial measuring spoons, plus a 25 mL amount. The larger measures contain 50, 75, 125 and 250 mL amounts, comparing roughly to the imperial measuring cups.

● When measuring out flour and sugar, spoon flour into dry measure until heaping. With knife, level off top evenly without shaking or tapping ingredients. To measure brown sugar, pack firmly but lightly and level top.

Raspberry Jiggle Yogurt

1	can (12 oz/341 mL) frozen raspberry cocktail concentrate, thawed	1
1/2 cup	water	125 mL
3 tbsp	granulated sugar	50 mL
2	pkg (each 7 g) unflavored gelatin	2
1	container (750 g) plain yogurt	1
	Raspberries	

● In large measuring cup, combine raspberry concentrate, water and sugar. Transfer 1/2 cup (125 mL) to separate bowl; sprinkle gelatin over top. Let stand for 2 minutes.

● Meanwhile, in microwave, heat remaining mixture at High for 2 minutes or until almost boiling; stir into gelatin mixture to dissolve. Place in larger bowl of ice water for about 20 minutes or until room temperature. Whisk yogurt into juice until blended.

● Pour into eight 175 g yogurt containers or custard cups; cover with plastic wrap. Refrigerate for about 3 hours or until set. Serve with raspberries. Makes 8 servings.

VARIATIONS
● PEACH JIGGLE YOGURT: Replace raspberry concentrate with 1 can (12 oz/341 mL) frozen peach cocktail concentrate, thawed. Serve with sliced peaches.

● PINEAPPLE JIGGLE YOGURT: Replace raspberry concentrate with 1 can (12-1/2 oz/355 mL) frozen pineapple juice concentrate, thawed. Serve with pineapple tidbits.

● ORANGE JIGGLE YOGURT: Replace raspberry concentrate with 1 can (12-1/2 oz/355 mL) frozen orange juice concentrate, thawed. Serve with orange sections.

This is another kid-tempter that solves the problem of what's healthful to eat for breakfast, lunch, snacks and dessert. The bonus to fun food like this is the nutrient content — about a half serving of calcium-rich dairy products from yogurt.

Breakfast Drop Cookies

1 cup	100% bran cereal	250 mL
3/4 cup	milk	175 mL
1	egg	1
1/3 cup	packed brown sugar	75 mL
1/4 cup	vegetable oil	50 mL
1 tsp	vanilla	5 mL
1 cup	all-purpose flour	250 mL
1/2 cup	whole wheat flour	125 mL
2 tsp	baking powder	10 mL
1 tsp	cinnamon	5 mL
1/2 tsp	salt	2 mL
3/4 cup	shredded carrots	175 mL
3/4 cup	raisins	175 mL

● In bowl, combine cereal with milk; let stand for 10 minutes. Beat in egg, sugar, oil and vanilla.

● In large bowl, combine all-purpose and whole wheat flours, baking powder, cinnamon and salt; stir in carrots and raisins. Stir in cereal mixture just until moistened.

● Drop batter by rounded tablespoons (15 mL) onto lightly greased baking sheet; flatten slightly with fork. Bake in 400°F (200°C) oven for 15 minutes or until tops spring back when lightly touched. Let cool on baking sheet for 5 minutes; transfer to rack and let cool completely. Makes 24 cookies.

Cookies for breakfast sounds like a come-on, but these bran, carrot and raisin drops are wholesome — and great for packed snacks and lunches, too. Well wrapped, the soft, cakey cookies keep for a few days and can be frozen for up to 2 weeks.

Toasted Oats Muffins ▼

The Mahon family of Staffa, Ontario, grows and processes oats to produce toasty rolled oats, then sells them mail order by the bag. Included with the oats are recipes, like this very popular one for muffins.

2 cups	rolled oats	500 mL
2 cups	packed brown sugar	500 mL
2/3 cup	vegetable oil	150 mL
4	eggs	4
1 tsp	vanilla	5 mL
3 cups	all-purpose flour	750 mL
2 tsp	baking soda	10 mL
1 tsp	salt	5 mL
1 cup	raisins, chocolate chips or coconut (optional)	250 mL

● In bowl, pour 2 cups (500 mL) boiling water over oats; let stand for 20 minutes. Beat in sugar, oil, eggs and vanilla.

● In large bowl, whisk together flour, baking soda and salt. Pour oat mixture over top; sprinkle with raisins (if using) and stir just until moistened.

● Spoon into greased muffin cups. Bake in 350°F (180°C) oven for 25 minutes or until tops are firm to the touch. Makes 18 muffins.

TIP: If you like, sprinkle muffin tops with rolled oats before baking.

Breakfast Sausage Kabobs

1	sweet red pepper	1
8 oz	sausages (8 links)	250 g
	MUSTARD SAUCE	
2 tbsp	Dijon mustard	25 mL
1 tbsp	chopped fresh dill (or 1 tsp/5 mL dried dillweed)	15 mL
1 tbsp	water	15 mL
1-1/2 tsp	soy sauce	7 mL
Dash	hot pepper sauce	Dash

● Cut red pepper into 1-inch (2.5 cm) squares. Cut each sausage link in half. Alternately thread red pepper and sausage onto each of 8 short metal skewers; place on baking sheet. *(Kabobs can be prepared to this point, covered and refrigerated for up to 12 hours.)*

● MUSTARD SAUCE: Combine mustard, dill, water, soy sauce and hot pepper sauce; brush half over kabobs.

● Broil kabobs for 6 minutes; turn and brush with remaining sauce. Broil for 6 minutes longer or until browned. Makes 8 servings.

Grand with pancakes and applesauce on the weekend, these tasty sausage kabobs can be put together the night before, ready to be brushed with sauce and cooked in the morning.

Herb Scrambled Eggs in Pita with Fresh Salsa

1 tbsp	butter	15 mL
1	onion, chopped	1
1-1/4 cups	sliced mushrooms	300 mL
6	eggs	6
3 tbsp	water	50 mL
1/4 tsp	each salt and pepper	1 mL
3 oz	herbed cream cheese (Boursin or Rondelé), crumbled	75 g
2	pita breads	2
	SALSA	
1	large tomato, seeded and diced	1
2 tbsp	chopped fresh parsley	25 mL
1 tbsp	olive oil	15 mL
1/4 tsp	pepper	1 mL
Pinch	salt	Pinch

● SALSA: In bowl, combine tomato, parsley, oil, pepper and salt; set aside.

● In large nonstick skillet, melt butter over medium heat; cook onion, stirring occasionally, for 3 minutes or until softened. Add mushrooms; cook for 3 to 5 minutes or until liquid has evaporated.

● Whisk together eggs, water, salt and pepper just until combined; add to skillet and cook, stirring, for 3 minutes or until softly set. Stir in cheese; cook for 1 minute or until beginning to melt.

● Meanwhile, halve pitas; pull open to form pockets. Divide egg mixture among pockets; top with salsa. Makes 4 servings.

If you're looking for speed and convenience in meal preparation, be sure to keep herbed cream cheese handy — it contributes fresh flavors and creaminess all at once. Stir it into scrambled eggs, then top with seasoned fresh tomatoes to create a cheesy dish that has eye and taste appeal to the max.

Sunny Spring Omelette ◄

2	eggs	2
2 tsp	water	10 mL
Pinch	each salt and pepper	Pinch
2 tsp	butter	10 mL
	Filling (recipes follow)	

● In bowl, stir together eggs, water, salt and pepper just until blended but not frothy. In 8-inch (20 cm) nonstick skillet, heat butter over medium-high heat until foaming, tilting to coat bottom and sides.

● Pour in egg mixture. Shaking pan and using underside of fork, stir eggs for 10 seconds. Cook, shaking pan occasionally and using spatula to push cooked eggs to center and let uncooked eggs flow underneath (tipping pan if necessary), for 40 to 60 seconds longer or until creamy but not liquid and bottom is light golden.

● Tilt handle up and shake pan to slide omelette up opposite side of pan. Spoon filling across center of omelette. Using spatula, fold one-third of the omelette closest to handle over filling. Lift/roll filled part of omelette over remaining uncovered omelette. Slide omelette, seam side down, onto plate. Makes 1 serving.

FILLINGS

● ASPARAGUS: Snap off ends from 6 stalks asparagus; cut stalks into 1-inch (2.5 cm) lengths. Steam or boil for 2 to 5 minutes or until tender-crisp; drain. Toss with 1/4 cup (50 mL) freshly grated Parmesan, and pepper to taste.

● MUSHROOM: In small skillet, cook 1 cup (250 mL) sliced mushrooms and 1 tbsp (15 mL) minced onion in 1 tbsp (15 mL) butter over medium heat for 3 to 5 minutes or until tender. Stir in 2 tbsp (25 mL) whipping cream; cook, stirring, for 1 minute or until slightly thickened. Stir in 1 tbsp (15 mL) chopped fresh parsley. Season with salt and pepper to taste.

● CHEDDAR AND SALSA: Combine 1/4 cup (50 mL) finely shredded Cheddar or Monterey Jack cheese, 2 tbsp (25 mL) salsa and 2 tbsp (25 mL) chopped green onion.

Omelettes move from tricky to easy-enough-for-a-novice with this recipe and a nonstick pan. Filled with asparagus, mushrooms or south-of-the-border salsa and Cheddar, omelettes quickly solve the problem of what to serve for a small weekend brunch or weeknight supper.

TIPS

● To lighten up an omelette, substitute 2 egg whites for one of the eggs.
● To make a perfect omelette, use a nonstick pan or one that has been seasoned by heating a thin layer of vegetable oil over medium-high heat for 5 minutes. Let cool and wipe out with paper towel. Do not wash seasoned pan with detergent. Instead, rub it with salt, then wipe out with clean towel.

EGGS FOR EASE AND SPEED

Eggs — there's no other ingredient that's so handy for quick and easy meals any time of the day.
● In moderation, nutrient-dense eggs can be a wholesome part of a healthy person's diet. One or two eggs are an alternate to meat and poultry in Canada's Food Guide to Healthy Eating.
● Like meat, poultry and seafood, eggs need to be cared for properly. Buy eggs from refrigerated cases and use before expiry date. Store in the carton in the coldest part of the refrigerator — never in the door which is subject to temperature fluctuations every time the refrigerator is opened. Since egg shells absorb odors, store eggs away from strong-smelling foods such as onions.

Baked Eggs and Spuds ▼

Cheap, cheerful — and especially handy for meals near the end of the week when the crisper and cupboard are registering close to empty.

4	large potatoes	4
1 tbsp	butter	15 mL
1	onion, chopped	1
Half	sweet green pepper, chopped	Half
1 cup	chopped mushrooms	250 mL
1 cup	shredded Cheddar cheese	250 mL
1/2 cup	diced cooked ham	125 mL
8	small eggs	8

● Scrub potatoes; pierce in several places. Bake in 400°F (200°C) oven for about 45 minutes or until tender. Cut in half lengthwise and scoop out flesh, leaving 1/2-inch (1 cm) thick shell and saving flesh for another use. Set shells in greased 13- x 9-inch (3 L) flameproof baking dish.

● Meanwhile, in small skillet, melt butter over medium-low heat; cook onion, green pepper and mushrooms, stirring occasionally, for about 10 minutes or until tender and juices have evaporated.

● Spoon half of the Cheddar into potato shells; top with mushroom mixture. Sprinkle with ham; top each with egg and sprinkle with remaining Cheddar. Bake in 400°F (200°C) oven for 8 to 10 minutes or until eggs are almost set. Broil for 2 minutes. Makes 4 servings.

Quick Western Sandwich

1 tbsp	butter	15 mL
1/2 cup	sliced mushrooms	125 mL
Half	sweet green pepper, diced	Half
1/2 cup	diced cooked ham	125 mL
1	green onion, chopped	1
Half	tomato, diced	Half
4	eggs	4
1/4 tsp	dried basil	1 mL
Pinch	each salt and pepper	Pinch
8	slices buttered toast	8

● In nonstick skillet, melt butter over medium-high heat; cook mushrooms, green pepper, ham and onion, stirring occasionally, for about 3 minutes or until vegetables are slightly tender. Add tomato; cook just until heated through.

● In bowl, whisk together eggs, basil, salt and pepper; pour over vegetable mixture. Run spatula around edge; cook for about 5 minutes or until eggs are almost set on top.

● Remove from heat; let stand for 3 minutes or until eggs are completely set. Cut into quarters; sandwich each between 2 slices of toast. Makes 4 servings.

"Western" in eastern Canada, "Denver" in the West, this green pepper, ham and mushroom sandwich is said to be Chinese in origin — the café version of egg foo yong turned into a toasted sandwich. Multigrain bread is recommended for its higher fiber and nutrient content.

Kids' Wings

1 lb	chicken wings	500 g
1/2 cup	all-purpose flour	125 mL
1 tbsp	wheat germ	15 mL
1-1/2 tsp	paprika	7 mL
1/2 tsp	each dried marjoram, dry mustard and salt	2 mL
1/4 tsp	pepper	1 mL
1/4 cup	buttermilk	50 mL

● Separate wings at joints, reserving tips for stock or soup. Line baking sheet with foil; grease foil.

● In plastic bag, shake together flour, wheat germ, paprika, marjoram, mustard, salt and pepper. Pour buttermilk into shallow dish.

● In batches, shake wings in flour mixture, shaking off excess back into bag. Dip into buttermilk; shake again in flour mixture. Arrange on prepared baking sheet.

● Bake in 400°F (200°C) oven, turning once, for about 35 minutes or until golden brown. Makes 14 pieces.

TIPS

● To be efficient, double the wing recipe and serve some for supper the night before. Pack the remainder for lunch the next day.

● If buttermilk is unavailable, combine 1/4 cup (50 mL) milk with 1 tsp (5 mL) vinegar; let stand for 15 minutes.

When kids graduate from peanut butter, here's a popular way to satisfy the lunchbox crowd. Pack these crunchy wings along with carrot and celery sticks, a fruity yogurt and an apple — and be sure to include a small freezer pack to keep food cold.

Minestrone Salad

Here's a delicious new take on pasta, vegetables and beans that's great for a supper side dish one night and for packed or home lunches the next.

1 cup	macaroni	250 mL
1/3 cup	olive oil	75 mL
1/3 cup	white wine vinegar	75 mL
1/4 cup	chopped fresh parsley	50 mL
1/4 cup	water	50 mL
1-1/2 tsp	dried basil	7 mL
1/2 tsp	each salt, pepper and granulated sugar	2 mL
1	can (14 oz/398 mL) red kidney beans, drained and rinsed	1
2	each carrots and small zucchini, thinly sliced	2
1 cup	each sliced celery and diced sweet red pepper	250 mL
1/2 cup	freshly grated Parmesan or shredded Jarlsberg cheese	125 mL

● In large pot of boiling salted water, cook macaroni for 8 to 10 minutes or until tender but firm; drain well.

● In large bowl, whisk together oil, vinegar, parsley, water, basil, salt, pepper and sugar; stir in warm macaroni to coat well.

● Add kidney beans, carrots, zucchini, celery, red pepper and Parmesan; toss to combine. Makes 6 servings.

Turkey and Cream Cheese on Rye

Post-holiday turkey or anytime chicken gets a flavor burst from herbed cream cheese.

4 oz	light cream cheese, softened	125 g
2 tbsp	chopped fresh parsley	25 mL
1 tbsp	chopped green onion	15 mL
1 tbsp	light sour cream	15 mL
1/2 tsp	dried tarragon	2 mL
Pinch	each salt and pepper	Pinch
8	slices rye bread	8
8	slices turkey	8

● In small bowl, beat together cream cheese, parsley, onion, sour cream, tarragon, salt and pepper.

● Spread on one side of each slice of bread. Top half of the slices with turkey; sandwich with remaining slices. Makes 4 servings.

Turkey with Creole Mayonnaise

Dills add crunch to a winning turkey and tingly mayo combo.

1/4 cup	light mayonnaise	50 mL
2 tbsp	minced green onion	25 mL
2 tsp	Dijon mustard	10 mL
1/2 tsp	vinegar or lemon juice	2 mL
	Black and cayenne peppers	
4	crusty rolls, split	4
8	thin slices roast turkey	8
2	large dill pickles, thinly sliced	

● In small bowl, stir together mayonnaise, onion, mustard, vinegar, and black and cayenne peppers to taste; spread on cut sides of rolls. Top half with turkey; arrange pickles over top. Sandwich with remaining halves. Makes 4 servings.

Micro-Melt Ham and Hot Pepper Sandwich ▲

2 tbsp	hot pepper jelly	25 mL
2	thick slices sourdough or Italian bread, toasted	2
4	thin slices Cheddar cheese	4
2 oz	thinly sliced black Forest ham	50 g

● Spread jelly over one side of each toast; top with Cheddar. Top one of the slices with ham; sandwich with remaining slice.

● Wrap in paper towel; microwave at High for about 1 minute or until Cheddar has melted. Makes 1 serving.

Pep up workplace lunches with something new and interesting to heat up in the microwave. Add roasted red peppers, if desired.

Lentil and Mushroom Soup

When planning weekend meals, a satisfying soup like this one is a great idea. Save any leftovers for hot Thermos lunches early in the week.

3	slices bacon, diced	3
1	each onion, carrot and stalk celery, chopped	1
3 cups	sliced mushrooms	750 mL)
2	cloves garlic, minced	2
1-1/2 cups	dried green lentils	375 mL
5 cups	chicken stock	1.25 L
1/2 tsp	each dried rosemary and thyme	2 mL
1/2 tsp	each salt and pepper	2 mL
Pinch	hot pepper flakes	Pinch
1	bay leaf	1
1/4 cup	chopped fresh parsley	50 mL
2 tbsp	lemon juice	25 mL

● In large saucepan, cook bacon over medium heat until crisp; remove to paper towel.

● Add onion, carrot and celery to saucepan; cook over medium-low heat, stirring occasionally, for 10 minutes. Add mushrooms and garlic; cook, stirring often, for 3 minutes.

● Meanwhile, sort and rinse lentils, discarding any blemished ones. Add to pan along with chicken stock, 2 cups (500 mL) water, rosemary, thyme, salt, pepper, hot pepper flakes and bay leaf; bring to boil.

● Reduce heat, cover and simmer for about 45 minutes or until lentils are tender. Discard bay leaf. Stir in parsley, lemon juice and reserved bacon. Makes 8 servings.

TIP: When deciding how many mushrooms to buy, remember that 1 lb (500 g) provides about 6 cups (1.5 L) sliced mushrooms.

Bacon and Egg Chowder

Cooking is always easier if you don't have to pick up exotic ingredients. Familiar ones help give this soup great mid-day satisfaction.

5	strips bacon	5
2	stalks celery (with leaves), chopped	2
2	each potatoes and carrots, diced	2
1	onion, chopped	1
1 tsp	dry mustard	5 mL
1 tsp	Worcestershire sauce	5 mL
3/4 tsp	dried marjoram	4 mL
1/4 tsp	salt	1 mL
Pinch	pepper	Pinch
2 tbsp	all-purpose flour	25 mL
3 cups	milk	750 mL
1 cup	chicken stock	250 mL
4	hard-cooked eggs	4

● In large saucepan, cook bacon over medium-high heat until crisp; crumble and set aside.

● Pour off all but 2 tbsp (25 mL) fat from pan; reduce heat to medium. Add celery, potatoes, carrots, onion, mustard, Worcestershire sauce, marjoram, salt and pepper; cook, stirring occasionally, for 5 minutes.

● Stir in flour; cook, stirring, for 1 minute. Add milk and stock; bring to boil. Reduce heat, cover and simmer for 10 to 15 minutes or until vegetables are tender.

● Remove whites from yolks and coarsely chop; add to soup and gently heat through. Finely chop yolks; sprinkle along with bacon over each serving. Makes 6 servings.

Nacho Soup

1 tbsp	vegetable oil	15 mL
1	onion, chopped	1
1	clove garlic, minced	1
1 tsp	chili powder	5 mL
1/2 tsp	each ground cumin and dried oregano	2 mL
1	can (28 oz/796 mL) tomatoes	1
2-1/2 cups	chicken stock	625 mL
1	can (19 oz/540 mL) red kidney beans, drained and rinsed	1
1	can (7 oz/200 mL) corn kernels	1
Dash	hot pepper sauce	Dash
1 cup	shredded Cheddar cheese	250 mL

● In heavy saucepan, heat oil over medium heat; cook onion, garlic, chili powder, cumin and oregano, stirring often, for 4 minutes or until onion is softened.

● Add tomatoes, breaking up with fork; pour in stock and bring to boil. Reduce heat and simmer for 20 minutes.

● Stir in beans, corn and hot pepper sauce; heat through. Serve sprinkled with Cheddar. Makes 6 servings.

Handy canned beans are the basis for this hearty soup, an ideal meal to simmer for Saturday lunch. Serve with nacho chips or tortillas warmed in the oven.

QUESADILLA COMBOS

Quesadillas are new-generation grilled cheese sandwiches. You start with tortillas, add cheese, nuts, veggies, beans, pesto — you name it — then fold over, toast on the grill until the cheese melts, cut into wedges and enjoy. Here are four great combos to spread over half of 4 (10-inch/25 cm) tortillas.

● **Trendy Tastes:** Spread with 4 oz (125 g) creamy goat cheese; sprinkle with 1/4 cup (50 mL) slivered roasted sweet red pepper or sun-dried tomatoes, 1 sliced green onion and 1/4 cup (50 mL) quartered black olives.

● **Fiesta:** Spread with 1/2 cup (125 mL) cooked and mashed red kidney beans; sprinkle with 1 cup (250 mL) shredded Monterey Jack cheese, 2 minced jalapeño peppers and 2 tbsp (25 mL) chopped fresh coriander.

● **Oozing Brie Pecan:** Cover with 4 oz (125 g) sliced Brie cheese; sprinkle with 1/2 cup (125 mL) chopped pecans and 1/4 cup (50 mL) shredded Gruyère cheese.

● **Pesto Pizza:** Spread with 1/4 cup (50 mL) pesto; sprinkle with 1 cup (250 mL) diced sweet green or yellow pepper, 1 seeded and diced tomato, 1/2 cup (125 mL) shredded mozzarella cheese and 2 tbsp (25 mL) quartered black olives.

The Contributors

For your easy reference, we have included an alphabetical listing of recipes by contributor.

Claire Arfin
Breakfast Sausage
    Kabobs, 81
Grilled Sirloin with Roasted
    Garlic Aioli, 54
Thai-Style Chicken, 56

Elizabeth Baird
Baked Eggs and Spuds, 84
Easy Pad Thai, 47
Nacho Soup, 89
Pesto Chicken Pasta
    Salad, 55
Quesadilla Combos, 89
Roasted Tomato Penne, 32
Salmon Patties, 26
Spicy Noodle Salad, 34
Strawberry Crème Brûlée, 63
Warm Caesar Salad Pasta, 33

Karen Barnaby
Piña Colada Fool, 62

Nancy Enright
Baked Italian Fish, 28
Shell Pasta with Vegetables
    and Clams, 33

Carol Ferguson
Crème Anglaise, 68

Margaret Fraser
Chocolate Fudge
    Pudding, 64

Joanne Good and Cynny Willet
Autumn Cobbler, 67

Jurgen Gothe
Pan-Fried Black Cod
    Fillets, 47

Barb Holland
Microwave Beef-Topped
    Tostadas, 16

Anne Lindsay
Chicken with Cumin and
    Garlic, 57
Mexican Pork Loin Roast, 48
Pacific Rim Flank Steak, 53
Spicy Scallops, 44
Upside-Down Apple
    Pancake, 76

Karen Mahon
Toasted Oats Muffins, 80

Beth Moffatt
Baked Summer-Fruit
    Compote, 58
Blueberry Frozen Yogurt, 63
Fresh Berry Pudding, 65
Lemon Mint Sauce, 69
Vanilla Custard Yogurt
    Sauce, 68

Rose Murray
Bacon and Egg Chowder, 88
Beef and Vegetable Stir-Fry
    For One, 9
Chicken with Hot Peanut
    Sauce For One, 20
Curry-Lime Barbecue Roast
    Chicken, 56
Kids' Wings, 85
Lentil and Mushroom
    Soup, 88
Micro-Melt Ham and Hot
    Pepper Sandwich, 87
Minestrone Salad, 86
On-the-Barbecue Onion Pot
    Roast, 54
Peppered Leg of Lamb, 52
Salmon and Potato
    Strata, 27
Tortellini Soup with
    Peas, 39
Turkey and Cream Cheese
    on Rye, 86
Turkey with Creole
    Mayonnaise, 86

Veggie-Stuffed Baked Potato
    For One, 37

Daphna Rabinovitch
Lean and Saucy Swiss
    Steak, 10
Roast Pork with Fennel and
    Garlic, 48
Steak Pizzaiola, 10
White Bean Spread and Pita
    Crisps, 40

Iris Raven
Broiled Peaches with Frozen
    Yogurt, 60
Chicken Stew For Two, 20
Lamb Curry, 15
Lightly Spiced Squash
    Gumbo, 39
Peppered Yogurt Cheese, 43
Roasted Pepper and Tomato
    Spread, 42
Touch of Thai Seafood
    Soup, 38

Linda Stephen
Cider-Baked Ribs, 50
Tuna Melt Pitas, 43

Bonnie Stern
Banana Nut Sauce, 78
Herb Scrambled Eggs in Pita
    with Fresh Salsa, 81
Shrimp Fried Rice, 26
Winter Fruit Crisp, 67
Whole Wheat Waffles, 78

Joanne Yolles
Honey Almond
    Nectarines, 58
Individual Summer
    Puddings, 63
Melon with Lime and
    Mint, 60

Canadian Living Test Kitchen

Almond Trout, 28
Apple Berry Clafouti, 65
Asparagus Pasta Toss, 30
Banana Brittle Sundaes, 62
Banana Split Ice Cream
    Cake, 71
Best Pancake Mix, 76
Best-Ever Pancakes, 74
Breakfast Drop Cookies, 79
Burgerbobs in a Bun, 15
Cardamom Chicken, 25
Cheesy Sloppy Joe Pizza, 36
Chick-Pea Burgers, 13
Chicken Satay, 21
Chili Meat Loaf Muffins, 17
Chili Salad with Lots of
    Vegetables, 34
Chocolate Raspberry
    Mousse, 64
Chops on the Grill, 48
Cinnamon Tortillas with
    Strawberry Salsa, 77
Confetti Chicken Meat
    Loaf, 23
Cranberry Coffee Cake, 69
Creamy Broccoli Pasta, 31

Dill-Grilled Salmon, 46
Friday Night Family
    Pizza, 35
Fruited Pork Chops with
    Squash, 18
Ginger Shrimp on Oriental
    Noodles, 44
Glazed Pork Tenderloin, 50
Healthy Processor Pizza
    Crust, 35
Herbed Quark Spread, 40
Honey Cardamom Coffee
    Cake, 72
Lazy Lasagna Toss, 30
Lemony Chicken
    Burgers, 13
Mango Fool, 62
Marble Chocolate
    Brownies, 72
Marinated Lamb Kabobs, 52
Mellow Liver and
    Onions, 17
Mocha Ricotta Cake, 71
Onion and Potato Pizza, 37
Oven-Baked Curried
    Chicken Legs, 23
Pancake Sandwiches, 74
Peppers Aplenty Pork
    Chops, 18

Quick Chicken and
    Mushrooms in a
    Skillet, 21
Quick Western
    Sandwich, 85
Raspberry Jiggle Yogurt, 79
Rhubarb and Berry
    Compote, 61
Rhubarb Fool, 61
Sesame Chicken, 24
Slice-and-Bake Almond
    Crisps, 68
Smiley Freezer Pizza, 36
Snacking Pizza, 37
Spanish Omelette Tapas, 43
Steak and Harvest Vegetable
    Fajitas, 6
Stewed Rhubarb, 61
Sticky Pineapple Ribs, 51
Strawberry Icebox Cake, 69
Sunny Spring Omelette, 83
Tangy Chicken Livers, 25
Teriyaki Pork Burgers, 12
Peanut Butter Tortilla
    Roll-Ups, 77

Photography Credits

LAURA ARSIE:
photo of Elizabeth Baird.

FRED BIRD: back cover (top
inset), pages 7, 11, 14, 16,
22, 24, 27, 35, 42, 45, 50, 53,
57, 59, 60, 65, 76, 82.

DOUG BRADSHAW: pages
36, 46, 49.

CHRISTOPHER
CAMPBELL: pages 4, 12, 32,
75, 89.

CHRISTOPHER DEW:
photo of Test Kitchen staff.

PAT LACROIX: page 73.

MICHAEL MAHOVLICH:
pages 19, 29, 31, 41, 87.

MICHAEL VISSER:
pages 51, 66, 84.

MICHAEL WARING: page 9.

ROBERT WIGINGTON:
front cover, back cover
(bottom inset), pages 4, 38,
70, 80.

Special Thanks

Canadian Living's Best series grows with the Spring 1995 titles, enriched with new contributors, and steadied by the experienced hand of project editor Wanda Nowakowska, Canadian Living's senior editor, Beverley Renahan, and Test Kitchen director Daphna Rabinovitch. All have contributed their expertise and attention to detail to every page. In the Test Kitchen, Dana McCauley created many of the new recipes, assisted by staff members Heather Howe, Jennifer MacKenzie, Kate Gammel and former staffers Jan Main and Donna Bartolini. Senior editor Donna Paris shaped many of the recipes when they first appeared in Canadian Living magazine.

We prize the delicious recipes created first by writers, especially our longtime contributors — Carol Ferguson, Marg Fraser, Beth Moffatt, Rose Murray, Iris Raven, Kay Spicer and Bonnie Stern — joined by writer and our nutrition editor, Anne Lindsay. We are thankful for the help of Olga Goncalves, Rosemary Hillary and Tina Gaudino who facilitate the works in

progress. Thanks go also to Canadian Living's art director, Martha Weaver, and former art director Deborah Fadden who have overseen almost all of the photography in this series. Our thanks to photographers Fred Bird, Doug Bradshaw, Christopher Campbell, Pat Lacroix, Michael Mahovlich, Michael Visser, Michael Waring and Robert Wigington for their luscious shots. Some new names have joined our food stylists, Olga Truchan and Jennifer McLagan; they include Claire Stancer, Ruth Gangbar, Debbie Charendoff Moses, Rosemarie Superville, Kathy Robertson and Sharon Dale. And when everyone else has finished arranging the recipes, the food, angles, props and lighting, book designer Gord Sibley puts the pages together so they're a treat to look at, but more important, easy to read and cook from. A heartfelt thanks and bravo to you all, and to Canadian Living editor-in-chief Bonnie Cowan and associate publisher Caren King. Their support of the Best series is valued.

Elizabeth Baird

Index

Over 100 delicious recipes — in no time at all!

A

Almonds
Slice-and-Bake Crisps, 68
Trout, 28

APPETIZERS
Herbed Quark Spread, 40
Peppered Yogurt Cheese, 43
Roasted Pepper and Tomato
Spread, 42
Spanish Omelette Tapas, 43
Tuna Melt Pitas, 43
White Bean Spread and Pita
Crisps, 40

Apples
Apple Berry Clafouti, 65
Cider-Baked Ribs, 50
Upside-Down Pancake, 76
Winter Fruit Crisp, 67
Apricots
Baked Summer-Fruit
Compote, 58
Fruited Pork Chops with
Squash, 18
Sticky Pineapple Ribs, 51
Winter Fruit Crisp, 67
Asparagus
Pasta Toss, 30
Sunny Spring Omelette, 83
Avocados
buying, 6
Steak and Harvest Vegetable
Fajitas, 6

B

Bananas
Banana Split Ice Cream
Cake, 71
Brittle Sundaes, 62
Fresh Berry Pudding, 65
Nut Sauce, 78
Peanut Butter Tortilla
Roll-Ups, 77

BARBECUE
burger basics, 12
Beef
Burgerbobs in a Bun, 15
Grilled Sirloin with Roasted
Garlic Aioli, 54
On-the-Barbecue Onion Pot
Roast, 54

Pacific Rim Flank Steak, 53
Chicken
Curry-Lime Barbecue
Roast, 56
Lemony Burgers, 12
Satay, 21
Thai-Style, 56
Fish
Dill-Grilled Salmon, 46
Lamb
Chops on the Grill, 38
Marinated Kabobs, 52
Peppered Leg, 52
Pork
Glazed Tenderloin, 50
Teriyaki Burgers, 12
Vegetarian
Chick-Pea Burgers, 12

Barley
cooking, 8
Bars and Squares
Marble Chocolate
Brownies, 72
Basil
Herbed Quark Spread, 40
Pesto Chicken Pasta
Salad, 55
Roasted Tomato Penne, 32
Bean Sprouts
Easy Pad Thai, 48
Spicy Noodle Salad, 34
Beans
Chili Meat Loaf Muffins, 17
Minestrone Salad, 85
Nacho Soup, 89
White Bean Spread, 40

BEEF
Ground
Burgerbobs in a Bun, 15
Cheesy Sloppy Joe Pizza, 36
Chili Meat Loaf Muffins, 17
Chili Salad, 34
Microwave Beef-Topped
Tostadas, 16
Liver
Mellow Liver and
Onions, 17
Roasts
On-the-Barbecue Onion Pot
Roast, 54
Steaks
and Vegetable Stir-Fry for
One, 9
Grilled Sirloin with Roasted
Garlic Aioli, 54
Lean and Saucy Swiss, 10

Pacific Rim Flank, 53
and Harvest Vegetable
Fajitas, 6
Pizzaiola, 10

Blackberries
Honey Almond
Nectarines, 58
Individual Summer
Puddings, 63
Blueberries
Baked Summer-Fruit
Compote, 58
Fresh Berry Pudding, 65
Frozen Yogurt, 63
Individual Summer
Puddings, 63
Bran
Breakfast Drop Cookies, 79
Broccoli
Creamy Pasta, 31
Brownies
Marble Chocolate, 72

BURGERS
basics, 12
Burgerbobs in a Bun, 15
Chick-Pea, 12
Lemony Chicken, 12
Salmon Patties, 26
Teriyaki Pork, 12

C

Cakes
Banana Split Ice Cream, 71
Cranberry Coffee, 69
Honey Cardamom Coffee, 72
Mocha Ricotta, 71
Strawberry Icebox, 69
Casseroles
Salmon and Potato Strata, 27

CHEESE
Cheddar
Baked Eggs and Spuds, 84
Baked Italian Fish, 28
Chili Salad, 34
Micro-Melt Sandwich, 87
Microwave Beef-Topped
Tostadas, 16
Nacho Soup, 89
Snacking Pizza, 37
Sunny Spring Omelette, 83
Tuna Melt Pitas, 43
Veggie-Stuffed Baked
Potato, 37

Cream
and Turkey on Rye, 86
Cranberry Coffee Cake, 69
Creamy Broccoli Pasta, 31
Herb Scrambled Eggs, 81
Other
Cheesy Sloppy Joe Pizza, 36
Chili Meat Loaf Muffins, 17
Friday Night Pizza, 35
Herbed Quark Spread, 40
Minestrone Salad, 86
Mocha Ricotta Cake, 71
Peppered Yogurt, 43
Ricotta, 30
Roasted Tomato Penne, 32
Smiley Freezer Pizza, 36
Warm Caesar Salad Pasta, 33

Chick-Peas
Burgers, 12
Lightly Spiced Squash
Gumbo, 39

CHICKEN
buying, 21
Breasts
Cardamom, 25
Pesto Pasta Salad, 55
Satay, 21
Stew for Two, 20
Thai-Style, 56
with Hot Peanut Sauce for
One, 20
Ground
Confetti Meat Loaf, 23
Lemony Burgers, 12
Legs, Thighs and Pieces
Oven-Baked Curried Legs, 23
Sesame, 24
Thai-Style, 56
with Cumin and Garlic, 57
with Mushrooms in a
Skillet, 21
Livers
Tangy, 25
Roast
Curry-Lime Barbecue, 56
Wings
Kids' Wings, 85

Chili
Meat Loaf Muffins, 17
Salad with Lots of
Vegetables, 34
Chocolate
Banana Split Ice Cream
Cake, 71
Fondue, 64
Fudge Pudding, 64
Marble Brownies, 72
Mocha Ricotta Cake, 71
Raspberry Mousse, 64
Clams
Shell Pasta with Vegetables
and Clams, 33

Cobblers and Crisps
Autumn, 67
Winter Fruit, 67
Cod
Baked Italian, 28
Pan-Fried Black Fillets, 47
Compote
Baked Summer-Fruit, 58
Rhubarb and Berry, 61
Cookies
Breakfast Drop, 79
Slice-and-Bake Almond
Crisps, 68
Corn
Cheesy Sloppy Joe Pizza, 36
Nacho Soup, 89
Shrimp Fried Rice, 26
Couscous
cooking, 8
Cranberries
Coffee Cake, 69
Curry
Curry-Lime Barbecue Roast
Chicken, 56
Lamb, 15
Oven-Baked Chicken
Legs, 23
Custard
Crème Anglaise, 68
Vanilla Yogurt Custard
Sauce, 68

D

DESSERTS
Baked
Apple Berry Clafouti, 65
Autumn Cobbler, 67
Winter Fruit Crisp, 67
Cold
Banana Brittle Sundaes, 62
Blueberry Frozen Yogurt, 63
Chocolate Raspberry
Mousse, 64
Mango Fool, 62
Piña Colada Fool, 62
Rhubarb Fool, 61
Strawberry Crème Brûlée, 63
Cakes
Banana Split Ice Cream, 71
Cranberry Coffee, 69
Honey Cardamom Coffee, 72
Mocha Ricotta, 71
Strawberry Icebox, 69
Cookies
Marble Chocolate
Brownies, 72
Slice-and-Bake Almond
Crisps, 68
Fruit
Baked Summer-Fruit
Compote, 58
Broiled Peaches with Frozen
Yogurt, 60

Honey Almond
Nectarines, 58
Melon with Lime and
Mint, 60
Rhubarb and Berry
Compote, 61
Stewed Rhubarb, 61
Puddings
Chocolate Fudge, 64
Fresh Berry, 65
Individual Summer, 63
Sauces
Chocolate Fondue, 64
Crème Anglaise, 68
Lemon Mint, 69
Vanilla Custard Yogurt, 68

Dips and Spreads
Herbed Quark, 40
Peppered Yogurt Cheese, 43
Roasted Pepper and
Tomato, 42
White Bean, 40

E

EGGS
buying and storing, 83
Apple Berry Clafouti, 65
Bacon and Egg Chowder, 88
Baked Eggs and Spuds, 84
Crème Anglaise, 69
Herb Scrambled, in Pita, 81
Quick Western Sandwich, 85
Salmon and Potato Strata, 27
Spanish Omelette Tapas, 43
Sunny Spring Omelette, 83

F

Fajitas
Steak and Harvest
Vegetable, 6

FISH AND SEAFOOD
Almond Trout, 28
Baked Italian, 28
Dill-Grilled Salmon, 46
Easy Pad Thai, 48
Ginger Shrimp on Oriental
Noodles, 44
Pan-Fried Black Cod
Fillets, 47
Salmon and Potato Strata, 27
Salmon Patties, 26
Shell Pasta with Vegetables
and Clams, 33
Shrimp Fried Rice, 26
Spicy Scallops, 44
Touch of Thai Seafood
Soup, 38
Tuna Melt Pitas, 43

Fools
Mango, 62
Piña Colada, 62
Rhubarb, 61

FRUIT. *See also listings under
individual fruit (e.g.* **Apples,
Bananas,** *etc.)*
Apple Berry Clafouti, 65
Autumn Cobbler, 67
Baked Summer Compote, 58
Chocolate Fondue, 64
Fresh Berry Pudding, 65
Individual Summer
Puddings, 63
Rhubarb and Berry
Compote, 61
Winter Crisp, 67

G

Garlic
Chicken with Cumin and
Garlic, 57
Grilled Sirloin with Roasted
Aioli, 54
Roast Pork with Fennel, 48
Roasted Tomato Penne, 32

H

Ham
Baked Eggs and Spuds, 84
Micro-Melt Sandwich, 87
Quick Western Sandwich, 85
Smiley Freezer Pizza, 36
Herbs
cooking with, 56
Quark Spread, 40
Scrambled Eggs in Pita, 81
Honey
Almond Nectarines, 58
Cardamom Coffee Cake, 72

I

Ice Cream
Banana Brittle Sundaes, 62
Banana Split Cake, 71

INFORMATION
Buying Chicken, 21
Cooking Barley, 8
Cooking Basics, 55
Cooking Couscous, 8
Cooking Kasha, 8
Cooking Pasta, 8
Cooking Polenta, 8
Cooking Potatoes, 8
Cooking Rice, 8
Cooking Terms and
Techniques, 55

Cooking with Herbs, 56
Eggs, 83
Measuring Dry
  Ingredients, 78
Measuring Liquids, 39
Preparing Peaches, 60
Ricotta Cheese, 30
Soy Sauce, 44
The Best Burgers, 12

Italian. See also Pasta and Pizzas.
Baked Fish, 28
Mocha Ricotta Cake, 71
Steak Pizzaiola, 10

K

Kabobs
Breakfast Sausage, 81
Chicken Satay, 21
Marinated Lamb, 52
Kasha
cooking, 8

L

Lamb
Chops on the Grill, 38
Curry, 15
Marinated Kabobs, 52
Peppered Leg, 52
Lasagna
Lazy Toss, 30
Lemon
Mint Sauce, 69
Lentils
and Mushroom Soup, 88
Lime
Chops on the Grill, 48
Curry-Lime Barbecue Roast
  Chicken, 56
Melon with Lime and
  Mint, 60
Thai-Style Chicken, 56
Liver
Mellow, and Onions, 17
Tangy Chicken, 25

M

Mango
Fool, 62
Meat Loaf
Chili Muffins, 17
Confetti Chicken, 23
Melon
with Lime and Mint, 60
Microwave
Beef-Topped Tostadas, 16

Micro-Melt Ham and Hot
  Pepper Sandwich, 87
Mousse
Chocolate Raspberry, 64
Muffins
Chili Meat Loaf, 17
Toasted Oats, 80
Mushrooms
and Lentil Soup, 88
Asparagus Pasta Toss, 30
Baked Eggs and Spuds, 84
Friday Night Family
  Pizza, 35
Herb Scrambled Eggs, 81
Marinated Lamb Kabobs, 52
Pan-Fried Black Cod
  Fillets, 47
Quick Western Sandwich, 85
Shrimp Fried Rice, 26
Sunny Spring Omelette, 83
Veggie-Stuffed Baked
  Potato, 37
with Chicken in a Skillet, 21

N

Nectarines
Honey Almond, 58
Noodles
Beef and Vegetable Stir-Fry
  for One, 9
Easy Pad Thai, 48
Ginger Shrimp on Oriental
  Noodles, 44
Spicy Salad, 34
Nuts. See also Peanut Butter.
Banana Nut Sauce, 78
Spicy Noodle Salad, 34

O

Oats
Toasted Muffins, 80
Winter Fruit Crisp, 67
Omelette
cooking, 83
Asparagus, 83
Cheddar and Salsa, 83
Mushroom, 83
Spanish Tapas, 43
Sunny Spring, 83
Onions
Mellow Liver and
  Onions, 17
On-the-Barbecue Pot
  Roast, 54
Onion and Potato Pizza, 37
Spanish Omelette Tapas, 43
Spicy Noodles, 30
Orange
Jiggle Yogurt, 79

P

Pancakes. See also Waffles.
Best Mix, 76
Best-Ever, 74
Sandwiches, 74
Upside-Down Apple, 76

PASTA
cooking, 8
Asparagus Toss, 30
Beef and Vegetable Stir-Fry
  for One, 9
Creamy Broccoli, 31
Easy Pad Thai, 48
Ginger Shrimp on Oriental
  Noodles, 44
Lazy Lasagna Toss, 30
Minestrone Salad, 85
Pesto Chicken Salad, 55
Roasted Tomato Penne, 32
Shell, with Vegetables and
  Clams, 33
Spicy Noodle Salad, 34
Tortellini Soup with
  Peas, 39
Touch of Thai Seafood
  Soup 38
Warm Caesar Salad, 33

Peaches
preparing, 60
Baked Summer-Fruit
  Compote, 58
Broiled, with Frozen
  Yogurt, 60
Jiggle Yogurt, 79
Peanut Butter
Chicken with Hot Peanut
  Sauce, 20
Tortilla Roll-Ups, 77
Pears
Autumn Cobbler, 67
Winter Fruit Crisp, 67
Peas
Shrimp Fried Rice, 26
Smiley Freezer Pizza, 36
Tortellini Soup, 39

PEPPERS
Aplenty Pork Chops, 18
Asparagus Pasta Toss, 30
Breakfast Sausage
  Kabobs, 81
Chili Salad, 34
Confetti Chicken Meat
  Loaf, 23
Easy Pad Thai, 48
Friday Night Family
  Pizza, 35
Marinated Lamb Kabobs, 52
Micro-Melt Sandwich, 87
Minestrone Salad, 85

Roasted Pepper and Tomato
  Spread, 42
Steak and Harvest Vegetable
  Fajitas, 6

Pesto
Chicken Pasta Salad, 55
Pineapple
Banana Split Ice Cream
  Cake, 71
Jiggle Yogurt, 79
Piña Colada Fool, 62
Sticky Ribs, 51
Pita Bread
Crisps, 40
Herb Scrambled Eggs in
  Pita, 81
Tuna Melt, 43

PIZZA
Cheesy Sloppy Joe, 36
Friday Night Family, 35
Healthy Processor Crust, 35
Onion and Potato, 37
Smiley Freezer, 36
Snacking, 37

Plums
Autumn Cobbler, 67
Baked Summer-Fruit
  Compote, 58
Polenta
cooking, 8

PORK
Chops
Fruited, with Squash, 18
Peppers Aplenty, 18
Ground
Easy Pad Thai, 47
Lazy Lasagna Toss, 30
Teriyaki Burgers, 12
Ribs
Cider-Baked, 50
Sticky Pineapple, 51
Roast
Mexican Loin, 48
with Fennel and Garlic, 48
Tenderloin
Glazed, 50

Potatoes
cooking, 8
Bacon and Egg Chowder, 88
Baked Eggs and Spuds, 84
Onion and Potato Pizza, 37
Salmon and Potato Strata, 27
Spanish Omelette Tapas, 43
Veggie-Stuffed Baked, 37
Puddings. See also Cobblers and Crisps.
Chocolate Fudge, 64
Fresh Berry, 65
Individual Summer, 63

Q

Quesadillas
Brie Pecan, 89
Goat Cheese, 89
Fiesta, 89
Pesto Pizza, 89

R

Raisins
Breakfast Drop Cookies,
Toasted Oats Muffins, 89
Winter Fruit Crisp, 67
Raspberries
Apple Berry Clafouti, 65
Chocolate Mousse, 64
Fresh Berry Pudding, 65
Individual Summer
Puddings, 63
Jiggle Yogurt, 79
Rhubarb
and Berry Compote, 61
Fool, 61
Stewed, 61
Ribs
Cider-Baked, 50
Sticky Pineapple, 51
Rice
cooking, 8
Chick-Pea Burgers, 12
Lamb Curry, 15
Shrimp Fried, 26
Roasts
Curry-Lime Barbecue Roast
Chicken, 56
Mexican Pork Loin, 48
On-the-Barbecue Onion
Pot, 54
Pork, with Fennel and
Garlic, 48

S

SALADS
Chili, with Lots of
Vegetables, 34
Minestrone, 85
Pesto Chicken Pasta, 55
Spicy Noodle, 34
Warm Caesar Pasta, 33

Salmon
and Potato Strata, 27
Dill-Grilled, 46
Patties, 26
Salsa
Chili Meat Loaf Muffins, 17
Cinnamon Tortillas with
Strawberry Salsa, 77
Herb Scrambled Eggs, 81
Snacking Pizza, 37
Sunny Spring Omelette, 83

SANDWICHES
Micro-Melt Ham and Hot
Pepper, 87
Pancake, 74
Quesadilla Combos, 89
Quick Western, 85
Turkey and Cream Cheese
on Rye, 86
Turkey with Creole
Mayonnaise, 86

Sauces
Banana Nut, 78
Crème Anglaise, 68
Lemon Mint, 69
Vanilla Custard Yogurt, 68
Sausages
Breakfast Kabobs, 81
Lazy Lasagna Toss, 30
Scallops
Spicy, 44
Touch of Thai Seafood
Soup, 38
**Seafood. See FISH AND
SEAFOOD.**
Shrimp
Easy Pad Thai, 48
Fried Rice, 26
Ginger, on Oriental
Noodles, 44

SOUPS
Bacon and Egg Chowder, 88
Lentil and Mushroom, 88
Lightly Spiced Squash
Gumbo, 39
Nacho, 89
Tortellini with Peas, 39
Touch of Thai Seafood, 38

Spreads. See Dips and Spreads.
Squash
Fruited Pork Chops, 18
Lightly Spiced Gumbo, 39
Steak
Beef and Vegetable Stir-Fry
for One, 9
Grilled Sirloin with Roasted
Garlic Aioli, 54
Harvest Vegetable Fajitas, 6
Lean and Saucy Swiss, 10
Pacific Rim Flank, 53
Pizzaiola, 10
Stews
Chicken, for Two, 20
Squash Gumbo, 39
Strawberries
Baked Summer-Fruit
Compote, 58
Banana Split Ice Cream
Cake, 71
Cinnamon Tortillas with
Salsa, 77
Crème Brûlée, 63
Fresh Berry Pudding, 65
Icebox Cake, 69
Rhubarb and Berry
Compote, 61

Rhubarb Fool, 61
Sundaes
Banana Brittle, 62

T

Teriyaki
Pork Burgers, 12

TEX-MEX
Chicken with Cumin and
Garlic, 57
Chili Salad with Lots of
Vegetables, 34
Cinnamon Tortillas with
Strawberry Salsa, 77
Mexican Pork Loin Roast, 48
Microwave Beef-Topped
Tostadas, 16
Nacho Soup, 89
Quesadilla Combos, 89
Steak and Harvest Vegetable
Fajitas, 6
Light Baked Taco Chips, 34

THAI
Easy Pad Thai, 48
Seafood Soup, 38
Thai-Style Chicken, 56

Tomatoes
Baked Italian Fish, 28
Cardamom Chicken, 25
Chili Salad, 34
Confetti Chicken Meat
Loaf, 23
Herb Scrambled Eggs, 81
Lean and Saucy Swiss
Steak, 18
Lightly Spiced Squash
Gumbo, 39
Nacho Soup, 89
Pesto Chicken Pasta
Salad, 55
Roasted Pepper and Tomato
Spread, 42
Roasted Tomato Penne, 32
Steak Pizzaiola, 10
Tortillas
Cinnamon, with Strawberry
Salsa, 77
Microwave Beef-Topped
Tostadas, 16
Quesadilla Combos, 89
Peanut Butter Roll-Ups, 77
Steak and Harvest Vegetable
Fajitas, 6
Taco Chips, 34
Trout
Almond, 28
Tuna
Melt Pitas, 43
Turkey
and Cream Cheese on
Rye, 85
with Creole Mayonnaise, 86

V

VEGETABLES. *See also listings
under individual vegetables (e.g.*
Asparagus, *etc.)*
Beef Stir-Fry, 9
Chicken Stew, 20
Chili Salad, 30
Shell Pasta with Vegetables
and Clams, 35
Shrimp Fried Rice, 26
Steak and Harvest Vegetable
Fajitas, 6
Touch of Thai Seafood
Soup, 38
Veggie-Stuffed Baked
Potato, 37

VEGETARIAN (Main Dishes)
Asparagus Pasta Toss, 30
Chick-Pea Burgers, 13
Creamy Broccoli Pasta, 31
Friday Night Family
Pizza, 35
Herb Scrambled Eggs in
Pita, 81
Onion and Potato Pizza, 37
Roasted Tomato Penne, 32
Snacking Pizza, 37
Spicy Noodle Salad, 34
Sunny Spring Omelette, 83
Veggie-Stuffed Baked
Potato, 37

W

Waffles
Whole Wheat, 78

Y

Yogurt
Broiled Peaches with Frozen
Yogurt, 60
Cardamom Chicken, 25
Fresh Berry Pudding, 65
Frozen Blueberry, 63
Mango Fool, 62
Peppered Cheese, 43
Raspberry Jiggle, 79
Strawberry Icebox Cake, 69
Vanilla Custard Sauce, 68

Z

Zucchini
Burgerbobs in a Bun, 15
Minestrone Salad, 86
Shell Pasta with Vegetables
and Clams, 33
Steak and Harvest Vegetable
Fajitas, 6

LOOK TO
CANADIAN LIVING
for all of
THE BEST!

only
$12.95

Over 100
all-new
recipes for
main dishes,
salads,
sauces and
soups

Canadian Living's™ best PASTA

FROM THE KITCHENS OF CANADIAN LIVING

Over 100
all-new
recipes for
perfect meals
around the
grill

Canadian Living's™ best BARBECUE

FROM THE KITCHENS OF CANADIAN LIVING MAGAZINE

Over 100
great-tasting
ways to
serve this
family
favorite

Canadian Living's™ best CHICKEN

FROM THE KITCHENS OF CANADIAN LIVING MAGAZINE

Over 100
all-new
fast and
fresh recipes
for healthy
eating

Canadian Living's™ best LIGHT COOKING

FROM THE KIT

Over 1
easy-baking
muffins, cookies,
snacking cakes,
squares and
quick breads

Canadian Living's™ best MUFFINS & MORE

FROM THE KITCHENS OF CANADIAN LIVING MAGAZINE

Over 100
satisfying
stews, soups,
casseroles,
stir-fries
and more

Canadian Living's™ best ONE-DISH MEALS

FROM THE KITCHENS OF CANADIAN LIVING MAGAZINE

Over 100
fast, easy
and delicious
recipes for
cooks on
the go

EASY COOKING

Canadian Living's™ best

FROM THE KITCHEN

VEGETABLES

Canadian Living's™ best

Over 100
recipes for
garden-fresh
entrées, salads,
side dishes
and soups

FROM THE KITCHENS OF CANADIAN LIVING MAGAZINE

WATCH FOR MORE NEW BOOKS IN
THE MONTHS AHEAD...
FROM *CANADIAN LIVING*
SO YOU KNOW THEY'RE —THE BEST!